The Election of Ideologies: Do You Know Where You Stand?

A Guide to the 2008 General and Presidential Elections

Marie Stacey

iUniverse, Inc.
New York   Bloomington

The Election of Ideologies:
Do You Know Where You Stand?

A Guide to the 2008 General and Presidential Elections

iUniverse books may be ordered through booksellers or by contacting:

iUniverse
1663 Liberty Drive
Bloomington, IN 47403
www.iuniverse.com
1-800-Authors (1-800-288-4677)

ISBN:978-1-4401-0024-6 (pbk)
ISBN: 978-1-4401-0025-3 (ebk)

Printed in the United States of America

Contents

Chapter One

Patriotism

I want to introduce this book in the best way that I know how – a call
to Patriotism. This book is a candid disclosure of facts about the current
United States government. I am going to discuss facts that I believe
are relevant to me and like-minded individuals to myself because it is
my right as an American to do so. If my opinions are unpopular and
criticized, then I have done a good job showing the opposition that
conservatives still exist in America, and we will still exercise our First
Amendment right to voice our concerns with the government candidly
and without regard to repercussions by oppositional views. Americans
can still act freely and decide for ourselves which topics we believe to
be relevant and which topics we intend to discuss to facilitate precise
and thoughtful debate.

I am an American. Aside from being a white female raised in the
South, I am an American first. My bloodlines include Italian, French,
and German blood, but I am an American. I love my Italian heritage,
but I am American. This country has given me the opportunity to
succeed, the opportunity to achieve, the opportunity to be free, and
the opportunity to be happy. I am forever grateful to this country.
It has given me more than I can ever give back to it. I am in awe of

the valiant men and women who have fought and given their lives to preserve the very freedoms I write about so passionately in this book. My grandfather served in World War II in the War in the Pacific. He spent months on a submarine fighting to defend his country against foreign invaders. He still remembers vividly the memories from the war and he still retains many of the ideals he gained serving in the military. He was a second generation Italian immigrant, but he will forever hang an American flag from his car's rear-view mirror. He is a true American. My father served in the Air Force. He also ultimately always desires for the well being of this country. My grandfather's brother was awarded the Silver Star for saving his entire platoon during World War II (Chapin). These men would have sacrificed anything to serve and defend their country including their lives. Life is the most important sacrifice and can only be made by the strong of heart and mind. These men fought for the freedom of every American to voice an opinion – be it unpopular, offensive to certain groups, or politically incorrect. The freedom to voice our concerns, our fears, and our worries without hesitation that we may be imprisoned for these beliefs. We shall not let the suffering and pain of war go unnoticed and unappreciated in this country. And we will remember what devotion to one's country means when we think of the men and women who have put their very lives on the line for the sake of the Constitution and for every man, woman and child to have the freedom to live without fear of foreign invasion.

Why are people not proud of this country anymore? Why did Michelle Obama say that she was 'proud of this country for the first time in her adult life' when Barack Obama was nominated for President? (Oinounou) That woman is quite audacious and misled to discredit all of the wars fought for the sake of justice, military involvement for the sake of human rights, the impact of World War II to disassemble Nazi Germany and blast Japan into oblivion for bombing Pearl Harbor. And Americans have always persevered. Those facts about this country make me proud to be an American. Americans have consistently and without regard fought for the sake of justice, freedom, and liberty. BE PROUD, Michelle Obama because the rest of the American public has taken pride in this country long before they knew your name and will continue to take pride in it long after you disintegrate out of the political realm.

Now, we have a decision before us that affects our very freedoms, the institutions that our fathers, grandfathers, and forefathers have fought and died for. We must value these decisions we make, especially for the President of the United States. This person will be critical to making decisions for and speaking on behalf of this country. We must critically analyze these candidates because if we do not, we are not true Americans. A true American cares so much for the well-being and the future of this country that they will not accept those who do not fight for the same ideals that are so embedded into their being. This is what being an American is all about.

I want every person that reads this book to take a moment to think about the opportunities that America has given to you. America is the best country on this earth. Do not let anyone convince you of the opposite. Americans know this, Europeans deny this, Middle Easterners despise this, and the Chinese understand this. Democracy and Capitalism has given this country the breath that no other country could ever suppress. The fire inside each one of us that drives us to succeed. In Economics, it is called incentive. Incentive has become a uniquely American phenomenon. We have revolutionized even the core meaning of the word incentive. Our economic progress has shown that incentive, as an internal motivator IS the most important economic devise for success. Other countries look to us, at our successes and failures, and they learn from our mistakes because they know that we are the most stable, civilized, economically prosperous nation in the world.

What is Patriotism? Patriotism as defined in the Merriam-Webster dictionary is 'love for or devotion to one's country.' But patriotism is personal and individual – it is molded by your experiences and your lifestyle. What are the memories that lead you to be patriotic? What does this word 'patriotism' mean to you? Now ask yourself which presidential candidate shows the most respect, love and devotion for his country.

Chapter Two

The indisputable facts

A brief glimpse into the lives of John McCain and Barack Obama

John Sidney McCain III was born in Panama Canal Zone on August 29, 1936 – which means he will be celebrating his 72nd birthday in August of 2008. He attended schools in Alexandria, Virginia and graduated from the United States Naval Academy in 1958. He also attended the National War college in Washington D.C. He served in the Vietnam War from 1958-1981 and was a prisoner of war in Vietnam from 1967-1973. He received various awards from his service including the Silver Star, Legion of Merit, Purple Heart, and Distinguished Flying Cross. He was elected as a House Representative to the Ninety-eighth Congress in 1982. He has been a member of the United States Senate representing Arizona since Jan. 3, 1991. He was also an unsuccessful candidate for the Republican presidential nomination in 2000. His Congressional experience begins with the 98th Congress and ends with the 110th Congress. All senatorial elections are dispersed into two-year voting blocks. (Washington Post)

Barack Hussein Obama was born in Honolulu, Hawaii on August 4, 1961. He attended schools in Jakarta, Indonesia of varying religious beliefs – including a Catholic school and a predominantly Muslim accredited Basuki School. (CNN) He also attended school in Hawaii. He completed his education at Occidental College in Los Angeles, California and Columbia University in New York City. He then proceeded to graduate magna cum laude from Harvard Law School where he became the first African American president of the Harvard Law Review. He worked as a professor of Constitutional Law at the University of Chicago. Barack Obama was elected to the United States Senate – 109th Congress -- in 2004 as a Democrat representing Illinois. His tenure in the Senate did not officially begin until January 3, 2005. (Washington Post)

A BRIEF SYNOPSIS OF SENATORIAL VOTING RECORDS OF BOTH CANDIDATES

"John McCain has missed 396 votes (63.2%) during the current Congress. [He] has voted with a majority of his Republican colleagues (88.3%) of the time during the current Congress."(Washington Post)

"Senator Barack Obama has missed 279 votes (44.5%) during the current Congress. [He] has voted with a majority of his Democratic colleagues (96.0%) of the time during the current Congress." (Washington Post)

John McCain has consistently voted supporting funding of the Iraq and Afghanistan wars. He consistently votes for bills concerned with funding the troops. Barack Obama has consistently voted in opposition to the War in Iraq since his induction into the Senate in 2005. On May 24, 2007, a proposition for Vote 181 passed through the Senate. The bill focused primarily on the funding of the Iraq War. The democrats had presented a previous bill demanding troop withdrawal dates, which the White House promptly vetoed. Barack Obama voted "No" when the White House sent this bill through the Senate because there were no deadlines for troop withdrawal. He clearly did not see the use in funding the military since he could not get his deadlines through. Vote 181 to fund the war in Iraq also included 18 "benchmarks that the Iraqi government must meet to continue receiving reconstruction aid." (Washington Post) Barack Obama voted in opposition to a Foreign Intelligence Surveillance Act – which passed regardless – but voted to extend a modification of the Patriot Act. I cannot understand why he would vote to extend the Patriot Act – which surveys American citizens – and vote against a Foreign Intelligence Surveillance Act – which intends to survey foreign terrorists or enemies. If he supports extensive surveillance of American citizens, why does he not support surveillance of potential foreign invaders? There are two other bills that Barack Obama and John McCain took opposing viewpoints on that are of particular interest. John McCain supported a proposed constitutional amendment that would give Congress the authority to ban 'desecration of the American flag.' Barack Obama voted "No" to this bill. I understand the argument Barack Obama will undoubtedly pose if questioned on this stance – he will argue it should be the freedom of the people to decide if they want to voice grievances within their country by any means they feel appropriate. There is no other reason that he would be in opposition to a bill banning the desecration of the flag. I think it is clear that the American flag means absolutely nothing to Barack Obama. Hence his displeasure at being expected to wear a flag lapel pin on his suit. I will admit that I don't know exactly what the argument is from the democrats on this issue of flag desecration, all I can say for certain is that their arguments are generally just namby-pamby, politically-correct liberal jargon. I just find it funny that liberal extremists only seem to fight for the freedom to hate your country, not to defend it. Barack Obama also voted "Yes" to a bill – Vote 307 -- expanding the State Children's Health Insurance Program. This program would increase funding to $60 billion dollars in $7 billion dollars per year increments. The funding for this program would come with a 61-cent increase in cigarette taxes. The Bush Administration vetoed this bill. John McCain also voted in opposition to this bill. John McCain voted "Yes" to cut nearly $40 billion dollars from the federal budget by "imposing substantial changes on welfare, child support and student lending programs." John McCain voted "Yes" on increasing the federal minimum wage from $5.15 an hour to $7.25 an hour over two years. "Minimum wage would be increased in 3 increments." Minimum wage is theoretically unnecessary in a Capitalist economy – I explain this theory in detail in the section of this book on "Ideologies Relevant to the Modern Era" the section on Capitalism (Washington Post Archives).

Chapter Three

An Overview of Ideologies Relevant to the Modern Era

In order to fully understand the policies of Barack Obama and John McCain, it is important to note the ideological differences between the two. It is important to understand the ideologies that form policy opinion. It is much easier to predict policy decisions in the future if ideological preferences are recognized. I will be referencing a text-book I got while studying at Wake Forest University called "Political Ideologies and the Democratic Ideal" by Terence Ball and Richard Dagger – 6th Ed., throughout this Chapter as it gives a somewhat comprehensive overview of the topics I intend to cover. I will not be quoting many specific excerpts from the book because I do not want to infringe on the copyright law, and I do not want to ask permission from the publishers of this text to cite a textbook I was obligated to purchase for an outrageous amount of money for a class. I also am extremely critical of this textbook throughout this chapter because it does not give an accurate and in-depth explanation of those ideologies that the authors do not particularly agree with – conservatism, neoclassical liberalism, libertarianism, and Capitalism. I will explain the thoughts of these

7

authors and the general basis of the textbook, but it will not be done in a positive light because it should not be. This is a textbook distributed to American universities and instead of defining Capitalism accurately and explaining the instrumental role of that form of government with the modern ideologies surrounding it, this book spends most of its time explaining the life and thoughts of Karl Marx, and a historical overview of Socialism, Communism, Fascism, Liberation Theology etc. I will be explaining Socialism, Marxism, Communism, Fascism, Stalinism, Ecology, Liberalism, and Conservatism, but I will be giving an accurate description of the downfalls of each form of government or ideological standpoint. The oppositional argument against Capitalism will be explained and logically disassembled by the end of this chapter.

Ideologies are a basis or set of beliefs that mirror a moral or ethical viewpoint on specific matters such as the freedom of the individual, class constraints in society, the interaction of human beings and animals, and appropriate solutions to the problems found in society. Ideologies usually utilize two main concepts in order to form a set of ideals: a defining idea of human nature and the concept of freedom, specifically how man can utilize the concept of freedom. Ideologies can incorporate thoughts on race, nationality, ethnicity, religious standpoints, government intervention, government control, moral and ethical obligations to mankind, and principle convictions. (p.2-4)

SOCIALISM

Socialism is an ideology that seeks to provide equality in the form of equal opportunity to the people contained in a society. Socialists largely believe that humans are social or communal beings by nature, and that human beings interact in ways that help each other and other members of society. Since individuals are not isolated from one another, socialists contend that members of society should be working for the common good or 'whole' of society. Socialists believe that humans cooperate with one another to complete their everyday tasks and therefore socialists should be compensated for these tasks in a way that addresses the instrumental role of every worker in producing the end-product of their labor. Socialists do not contend that human beings are competitive creatures, but that we are beings that should work in cooperation with one another regardless of our clearly competitive human nature. (p.115)

More precisely, Socialists believe that humans are communal creatures who work in cooperation and should therefore partake equally in whatever they produce. People, they believe, work similarly even if they are working different professions because the labor produced is valued over specialized interests. In socialism, the government sponsors production of critical industries, and in the words of Representative Maxine Waters: "this liberal – Barack Obama -- is all about socializing America...ahhh...errr...(pause) will be about (pause) basically taking over, and the government running all of your companies." They believe that businesses are more productive if strictly monitored and eventually taken over by the government because then they can dictate precisely how the country's businesses function and are maintained. Socialism is a diluted form of Communism in that it does not necessarily advocate full control of the government by one dictatorial body. Socialist ideas can also be implemented into an economy without a complete revamp of economic conditions. However, these policies over time will negatively affect the productivity of the economy if they are instituted into a Capitalistic economy that flourishes with innovation. Innovation is not as prized in a socialist community because all work is thought to be equal – regardless of the amount of extra specialization needed to complete some, more difficult and arduous tasks. People do not have the incentive that Americans have to produce and become more efficient for their own aspirations because they will forever be given the same wage or compensation for their job – no matter the amount of extra work that they put into it.

Socialism, in essence, discourages individuality – which is why I believe that it is illogical for Karl Marx to assert that Capitalism strips the proletariat or working class of individuality. That is simply a ludicrous assertion from the man that created Marxism – a critique of Capitalism that leads to a revolt and then Communism. Communism completely strips the individual of their specific interests and does not value individual freedom or liberty. The working class in this country has individuality in that they have the freedom to choose their own course in life. Monetary compensation by the government in America is not guaranteed to anyone, but the opportunities that individuals have every single day to succeed are unparalleled in these other socialist or Communist regimes. If an individual has a falling out with their employer and must leave their current job, then tomorrow they can open up the paper and look through the pages upon pages of private businesses offering positions to qualified individuals. It is not the businesses' fault if an individual is not qualified for a position. That mindset is just detrimental to positive development. Americans should strive to exceed expectations – not to merely be 'normal' like the rest of the population. And Americans have consistently exceeded expectations, which is why Karl Marx, Fredrick Engel, and others adhering to Marxist thought have so harshly criticized the Capitalist movement.

Note that socialists do not necessarily value traditions or customs rooted in American History. (p.115) But why not? The United States is a melting pot of every nationality on the planet, but why can Americans not have traditions and customs that are valued by every single American the way that cultures and traditions from other countries are valued by Americans? I understand that people feel tied to a specific nation of origin that their ancestors have come from. I'm a fourth generation Italian-American, and I love Italian customs and traditions; however, I understand that I am an American, and that my allegiance, gratitude, and success should be attributed back to MY homeland, not my ancestor's homeland. This country has given my family more opportunities than their own country ever could. That's why they came here. In the words of the departed Estelle Getty – (Sophia Patrillo), actress, Golden Girls; " It wasn't a pleasure cruise", but they knew that on the other side of that ocean was a land where their children and their children's children could live freely and make their own decisions on how their lives should be lived. Value your ancestor's decision to come to this country, and if they did not come on their own and were enslaved, then also give credit to the country that sold those people to the United States for the horrible treatment they endured during the era of slavery. America, no matter the argument, is not a land of injustice not rectified. Injustices are recognized, rectified, and then prohibited. That is a uniquely American tradition in that we can recognize these faults in ourselves and correct them, and Americans would do well to remember that.

Socialists install programs that will redistribute wealth and power to other members of society, this practice is also known as 'levelling.' They also believe that since members of society cooperate in order to create and produce goods and products for society, then the society collectively and not individuals should own property and control businesses. (p.15) However, history has shown that society – and more accurately, the government -- is much less efficient in handling business and property as compared with private individuals. Also, revoking the right to private property involves a staunch disregard of personal liberty and freedom. Individuals are not even free to own their own property in a socialist regime. They are not free to become an entrepreneur that invents and invests in themselves and then is able to reap the benefit of their ideas and innovation. This textbook fails to accurately address that 'society' does not own the property and businesses revoked from individuals, the government owns it. The government's elected or non-elected officials control the production of goods and the job market in their country, as well as all of the property in the country. When Socialism is utilized as a form of government and not merely an ideological standpoint, the products of this government can be directly linked to the product of a Communist government. Complete control by the government over individuals – supposedly for the 'common good.'

Socialists believe that 'once the fears of poverty and hunger and homelessness are banished, the foundations of greed and envy disappear.' And the result of this line of thinking, they believe, is utopia – a 'good or happy place' or 'no place.' Greed and envy are two factors that are predominant in a Capitalist society. It cannot be disputed because we have the free ability to make as much money as we want without regulation by the federal government. However, greed is not the only product of Capitalistic thought, nor is it the most prominent or dominant theory. Humans have flaws; that is something that socialists, Capitalists, Communists, and leftists alike must understand. Democrats should especially be able to understand this in light of the fact that John Edwards has now openly admitted to committing adultery against Mrs. Elizabeth Edwards who has now been diagnosed with an untreatable form of cancer. I am not going to speak about this at length because I cannot imagine the pain and heartache that Mrs. Edwards is having to endure right now, and it gives him too much credit to even mention his name more than twice in this book. He is a terrible man with a terrible agenda and absolutely no morals, so goodbye Edwards; I hope I never have to hear about you running for elected office again. Leftists, liberals, socialists, Communists and any other person who subscribes to the Democratic Agenda had better only carefully place so much emphasis on the negative effects of greed – because in my opinion, there are many other things that I have seen come out of the Democratic Party that are much more despicable than merely a single man's want for more money.

This is a brief overview of the tenants of socialism; I have not explained it in a way that Europeans will agree with, but this is an accurate overview of socialism from a Capitalist's perspective. Socialism is not an ideology that prides the individual's achievements in society, socialism values the 'whole' of society to work for the greater good of all members within it. They fail to notice that this is an extremely unreasonable expectation because people do not necessarily want to work for everyone else in society. I certainly don't. I am not expending my time, resources, and intelligence in order to fund the government's control over my property and my industries. That's a ludicrous mindset to me and many other Americans.

Marxism and Communism – Defining the Interrelationship Between the Two Ideologies

Before I begin giving an overview of Marxism and the ideals that have formed it, I would first like to point out a few things. Marxism purports to eliminate the class system or class constraints in society by methods of government control and socialization. It is important to note that Marx outlines a revolutionary attempt (discussed at length later) by the proletariat – or the working class, as he defines it – to form a new dictatorial, Communist regime. He believes this will be the end product of a Capitalist society that cannot understand the struggles of the working class. His doctrine mirrors both socialist and Communist ideals, as does Senator Barack Obama's. I will explain at the end of my explanation of Marxism the way in which I believe Senator Obama is reverently and irreversibly tied to this ideology. But remember, the end result of Marxism is Communism, for, as the Marxist believes, there is no higher form of equality than that found in a Communist regime. Also, many people that have utilized this ideology in their policy making platforms have done so on the basis that they would like to take the power from the current ruling class. So, in essence, if Barack Obama converts this country to Communism, he will be the dictator of this country. Marxism fails to account correctly that they are advocating not the absence of power, but a complete shift of power from one sector to another, and in this shift will come the loss of freedom of the individual – which they do not value. The bourgeoisie is the 'ruling' class, the capitalists in the economy – those individuals who strive to succeed in society while simultaneously overcoming struggle and adversity of their own along the way. Marxists do not value the lives of these people, nor do they think they have necessarily labored for the good of the others in their society. The proletariat is known as the working class. Bourgeoisie can also commonly be referred to as the middle class.

In Tier of the German Rhineland, Karl Marx was born in the year 1819. His father was a somewhat successful lawyer. Marx was forced to convert from Judaism to Christianity later in life because the government would not allow Jews to practice law. Marx attended the University of Bonn where he studied law and was a somewhat rambunctious student known for drinking heavily, debating politics, and fighting with some of his peers. (p.122)

I know this all sounds familiar to you. A learned scholar who was never impoverished – but endured religious persecution, which forced him to convert to Christianity. Barack Obama's keynote address is noted in the section of this book on 'Religion,' and can be viewed at length there; however, he mentions his upbringing and his later convert to Christianity for personal and political reasons.

Marx later moved toward a more revolutionary pattern of thinking when he abandoned liberalism and intended to create a revamp of an economic system he deemed to be so rotten that it would have to be completely re-mastered and re-formulated. (p.124) He then began a detailed overview of the flaws within a Capitalist form of government and how it will ultimately be converted to Communism via a revolt by the proletariat.

Marx was largely concerned with the history of humans' labor and struggle within society to maintain an autonomous relationship with one another. He believed the world to be hostile and believed that society persecutes the lowest class of people intentionally. He calls the interests of capitalists and the proletariat or 'working class' "diametrically opposed" – meaning that their interests and their successes are not linked together but are the opposite of one another. He believed that history told the story of the struggle of the lowest class system for survival. (p.126)

But humans, collectively, have always survived regardless of the adversity they have faced: be it weather-related, government-related, or socially-related. Americans specifically have overcome obstacles set in their path by this outdated form of negative thought. I also do not believe that capitalists and workers can be defined as diametrically opposed, as many capitalists, most even, are workers themselves. Capitalists, for the most part, do not start out on top. They must work those menial and trivial jobs that are unfavorable to them. The opportunities that have been bestowed on working Capitalists are not limited to an individual's personal wealth – it is contingent upon what the individual will do to excel. It annoys me endlessly the lengths that Marxists will go to stifle the achievements of capitalists in any realm. These achievements, innovations, or industries are of little to no relevance to Marxists because they are concerned only with convincing the proletariat to rise against the 'ruling' or middle class.

Marxists are not concerned with those who have spent their entire lives working to attain success and a comfortable lifestyle for themselves and their family They believe that wealth should be evenly distributed between those who partake in creating it. Essentially, the individual does not own anything that is specifically his or hers in a Communist regime. Workers must labor for the 'social or communal' good because Marxists believe that we are social and communal beings that would do better to realize the ways in which we help one another everyday.

Marxists fail to realize that there is a symbiotic relationship between worker and boss in this country. The boss cannot indefinitely oppress the worker, no matter the circumstance. That's why it is simply inconsistent with reason to ignore that the business owner and will do those things necessary to maintain the company; however, the individual worker's ability to perform the task at hand is compensated and appreciated by the business owner who knows that the business could not survive without employees to ensure its continued stability and prosperity. Capitalists, contrary to Marxist beliefs, do not believe that the government can fill their needs or wants, nor do capitalists trust the government to 'fix' societal constraints. History has shown that the government convinces the citizens that their intentions are only to eliminate poverty and the class system; however when absolute power corrupts, Marxists fall to their knees and embrace it as any good Communist or Dictator would. Americans must understand that Communism and specifically Barack Obama's form of Marxism will not yield a form of government controlled by the citizens, but a government controlled by a small group of parliamentary leaders who will decide the length and severity of government intervention in every facet of every day life. Freedom will be an obsolete ideal.

Marx believed that the proletariat is defined as those individuals forced by capitalists to transfer their labor to a private business solely for the profit of the capitalists. If you do not own the means of production, Marx believed that an individual had no option but to sell his/her labor to the capitalist for their benefit. (p.128) However, he completely ignores the fact that the laborer in a Capitalist society has the indefinite ability to say no to any job they do not believe is suitable for them, and they are compensated BY THE CAPITALISTS for performing the job. The proletariat is not oppressed by the business owner because without the business owner, there are no jobs for the working class. None at all. Not even ones that they do not particularly enjoy. Also, if Marxists would like to convince the American public of how oppressed they are, they will have a pretty hard time convincing anyone that the Constitution of the United States is oppressive. And if you think the United States is oppressive now, then wait until a Communist steps into office and revolutionizes (in an extremely unproductive way) the federal government. Americans do not understand oppression – definitely not in this country, leftists may purport to understand oppression in other countries or past injustices, but not a single American is oppressed by the federal government in this day and age. However, that can all change if we allow ourselves to be overthrown by Communists. Leftists will of course disagree with that statement, but they really have no rationale since it is NOT the job of the federal government to guarantee wages to any individual person. That is the individual person's responsibility – another Capitalistic ideal that Marxism gives absolutely no credit to. Personal responsibility is not utilized by Marxist thinkers because they would rather the public be dependent upon the government for their wants and needs rather than feel personally responsible for the life predicament they are in.

Marx notes that the working class is larger than what he deems to be the ruling class. Remember that the 'ruling' class is defined as the middle class in America. We do not have a 'ruling' class. We have a lower, middle, and upper-middle class, and we also have the government. The government, as outlined but not specifically stated in Marxist ideology, should be the ruling class. The government should dictate to individuals the jobs they should have, the amount of money they should be compensated for those jobs, and the government also dictates how much control over individuals that it desires. Marx attempts to define capitalists by a monetary figure or a salary; however, that is not an accurate description of Capitalists. Capitalists are not defined by the amount of money they have gained through their innovation and aspirations, they are defined as the individuals in this society that make it work. It really is that simple. Without capitalists, the United States of America would be a country of industrialization and factories and government control. Capitalists propel Americans to have a mindset for success and achievement; they do not stifle the working class, but they do encourage the working class to become truly educated and involved in the development of crucial industries and their own success.

Marx notes that capitalists control the 'agencies of coercion' – such as the police, military, prisons, and court systems. This is also an incorrect assessment of the Capitalist society in which we live. He incorrectly defines this as 'ruling class' control over the proletariat. Americans should be able to point out the flaw in his thought immediately. The capitalists do not control the police force, the judicial system, the military, the prisons; the government controls those industries in this country. I absolutely cannot understand why a man that defines Capitalism and Capitalists incorrectly time after time is taken seriously in the academic circles of this country. Marx is INCORRECT in his assessment of Capitalism. He makes blatant false statements about the form of government and then attempts to solicit those without the ability or courage to critically analyze his thoughts to believe his nonsensical rhetoric about Capitalism.

The thing that irritates me most about Karl Marx is that HE was a part of the middle class in his society. He was not impoverished and he was educated to some extent. I would not necessarily call him 'educated' in the sense that he actually knows and understands the full tenants of the arguments he's making against Capitalism, because he clearly does not, but he was educated European-style. Professors need to stop idolizing this man because he has done nothing productive for this country or even his own country. He gained fame and accolades by creating a method of overthrow of the American form of government. He proposes no unique solution. He proposes no unique line of thought even, as most of his thoughts and beliefs on Capitalism are inaccurate or fail to detail an appropriate version of the full ideological standpoint of Capitalism. Why must we learn about this man in American universities? I have learned his ideas and his thoughts, I understand the premise of his arguments, but I cannot understand why I was engrained these teachings in an American university. Professors need to understand that giving a description of Karl Marx and his thoughts is not detrimental, but failing to detail the shortcomings and misleading statements made by Marx about Capitalism IS detrimental to the development of fully formed opinions on these issues. Karl Marx was only a revolutionary man in that he encouraged a direct revolution in the United States of America by the working class. His ideals are not revolutionary. He created a method to install Communism.

Marx was also extremely cynical to religion calling it the "opium of the people." He laments on religion and says that 'it dulls [peoples'] minds and makes them uncritical of the wretched conditions in which they live.' (p.129) Marxism intends to alert people to their circumstance, as if they are not capable of knowing the ins and outs of their own lives without the help of an ideologue with a Communist agenda. It also gives people a weary outlook on their own abilities to succeed without having to have their hand held by the federal government.

Marxists consistently negate the effects of human nature and the sociology of human beings and animals. They do not believe in things such as 'survival of the fittest,' which can be found as a driving force in any ecosystem. They do not believe that the will of the individual to survive for one's self should be commended, but a collective effort toward the greater good of the society should be tried. Animals are also competitive, even in nature. FACT. Also, freedom is a threat to this ideological standpoint for a number of reasons: 1) Freedom is not an adherence of Marxist thought. Individual liberty is thought to be an unnecessary commodity of sorts. 2) They downplay the role of this critical function of the democratic republican government in America; however, they do not completely ignore it. They cite that the freedom to trade, the freedom to compete, and the freedom to make a profit without 'interference' from the government should all be demonized. They also put 'interference' into quotations since Communists/ Marxists advocate quite a bit of government interference in everyday life, but I'm sure they would rather skim over that fact rather than really addressing it when giving a positive summary of the Marxist ideals.

Karl Marx believed that the working class has been in a state of false consciousness – so oppressed by the capitalists that they are unable to gain a true and accurate picture of the life predicament they are in. He says that the proletariat takes these capitalists' ideas as their own and are brainwashed by these concepts. The proletariat cannot understand their own suffering and their own lifestyles because they are thought not to have been given this thought-process by the capitalists. I'm not sure why Marxists believe that those in the working class are incapable of critical and analytical thought, but I can assure you that that is an inaccurate assessment of the working class in the United States of America.

No matter the lengths that Obama has gone to pander to the American public, it is more than evident that he believes us to be inferior to him – without his breadth of knowledge and insight. I can never fully understand the Marxist standpoint since they consistently and without regard insult and degrade the proletariat (working class) stating that they are too ignorant or brainwashed to understand their own circumstance, yet they say the capitalists are the oppressors. I believe the oppressors, without a doubt, are the Communists who demean all progress made by the working class, and consistently make them feel as if they will never be able to succeed. If someone begins life in the proletariat, aspires to many more things, and in time succeeds in becoming part of the middle to upper-middle class then they are still demeaned by the Marxists. In fact, essentially every group of humans is somehow insulted or demeaned by the Marxists – who believe themselves to be above such class restrictions. An example of this would be Barack Obama's criticism of Supreme Court Justice Clarence Thomas (spoken about further in the section on Conservatism). Karl

Marx believes the working class to be in a state of 'false consciousness' brought about by the capitalistic goals of the bourgeoisie.

Marx does admit that capitalism, throughout history, has been a "progressive force for the good." But he believes that capitalism is 'outmoded, creates alienation, and is self-subverting.' But he goes on to note that "he is not criticizing capitalism on moral grounds, nor is he questioning the moral character of capitalists as individuals or even as a class."(p.131-132)

Marx also agreed that "[c]apitalists keep wages low not because they are immoral or cruel, but because the logic of the system requires them to do so." In one of his critiques of capitalism, he cites monopolies and small business loss as two reasons that capitalism does not benefit the working class. (p.132) Monopolies are well regulated in the United States and many preventative measures have been taken by the government to establish firm laws prohibiting monopolies from taking a disproportionate hold over the economy. These factors that concerned Karl Marx in the mid-1800's have been rectified somewhat in the last 150 years by strategic moves and intelligent capitalists looking toward progressive but stable change in this country. Small business loss is inevitable in a Capitalist economy; some businesses succeed, some fail. But a failed business venture does not mean that the American entrepreneur needs to throw in the towel or call it quits. The entrepreneur can wake up the next morning and begin a new business venture that could this time yield him a profit or make an outstanding investment. Opportunities come and go in Capitalism, but they are always present. People take that for granted. With the loss of a job comes the potential opportunity to find a job more suited for a person's specific interests. There will be none of that with Communism. Specialization, the ability of an individual to specialize in a specific interest or industry, cannot be accomplished in a Communist society – definitely not to the extent that it can be practiced and achieved with a Capitalist economy.

Marx believed that change would come about in a capitalist society moving to communism as the working class realizes that their role in society is not equal to the capitalist's.

Marx believed that '[a]fter all, it would be impossible – logically impossible – for everyone to become a capitalist.' First of all, no it is not impossible because being a Capitalist is a state of mind and not a monetary figure in a bank account. Second, it is also illogical to think that socialization of America to a Communist regime will yield a happy end-result for any Capitalist. Is that not important? Are the lives of Capitalists so unfortunate and misused that Marx must completely eliminate the call from the oppositional argument that states that Capitalists will logically never be able to be Communists? If Marx can assert without regard that it is illogical to believe that every person can become a Capitalist, then it is also logical to assert that not every Capitalist can become a Communist, and therefore, the argument is null and void as it stands. Americans would be forced into Communism because it is an ideology that pretends to accept everyone on equal grounds, but it also hampers any effort of the individual to be apart from the government or work apart from the government. I will logically never be able to be a Communist simply because it is not the most productive economic route for America, and I do not agree with the ideals set forth by Karl Marx, Friedrich Engel, and early Communists. So it is logically impossible for all Capitalists to become Communists; however, Communists could drag Americans kicking and screaming into that form of government and then pretend that they have converted us on the grounds that 'everyone can be a Communist because, well, you don't have to do anything at all to be a Communist except work for the greater good of the government.' That is not rational to Americans. Also, I would like to point out the distinction that Marx always makes between workers and capitalists. I know I've pointed that out before, but it needs to be noted again. Karl Marx did not fully understand a Capitalist society because he does not account for the pioneering work of the capitalists. Yes, Marx, WORK of the Capitalists. Karl Marx was a revolutionary man hell-bent on finding a 'solution' to Capitalism before he passed away; however, he did not. Marxism proposes no unique solution to problems; it proposes Communism, and of course, a revolution by the working class who may be the only group of individuals Marx will be able to convince with his crystalline logic stating that not everyone can be a Capitalist. Any one individual can be a capitalist at any time in their life if they so choose to be that way in the United States of America. Remember that, too, Americans.

Marx believed in a revolutionary sequence including seven different stages that would leave the end-result of Communism in a Capitalist state. First, he speculated, there would be an economic crisis in the region as he cites that economic growth always results somehow in a recession or depression, and with this recession or depression comes a renewed sense of despair and anger from the working class. Second, he believed in an 'immiseration of the proletariat' as their personal wealth and job security begin to ebb away in the face of recession. Third would be a revolutionary class-consciousness where the miserable class of the proletariat begins to blame the capitalists for their state in society stating that jobs do not exist for them even though they are willing to work – as if the American economy is not capable of producing jobs for individuals in the future. He then stated that in the fourth stage of revolution, spontaneous supposedly unrelated strikes, boycotts, and riots begin the revolution against the middle class, and as the revolution builds, the proletariat organizes into a militant force against the current 'ruling' class. He speculates on a number of different ways this can occur including 'a general strike that will cripple the economy and bankrupt the capitalists almost overnight. Another possibility is a bloody civil war pitting capitalists, soldiers, and police against armed proletarians.' Another unlikely possibility they state is that 'the bourgeoisie will be overthrown not by bullets but by ballots in a free and fair election.' Marxists do not contend that a free and fair election will be the way the Communist revolt strangleholds America, but Marx does agree that it is a possibility. In the fifth step of this process, 'having seized state power, the proletariat proceeds to establish what Marx called the revolutionary dictatorship of the proletariat.' The proletariat becomes the new ruling class. In the sixth step of the process, "Marx states that the proletariat's defeat of the bourgeoisie will inaugurate a transitional period that will take society from capitalism to full-fledged communism which is the seventh and final step. (pp.134-137)

Karl Marx did not live to see his ideologies and thoughts carried out, but, to this day, scholars are still entranced by the ideas he put forth – however flawed they may be, and some continue to engage in renewed efforts every couple of years or decades to implement these ideals, but Marxism does not suggest its own policy of government after the overthrow of Capitalism, it suggests Communism which has proven over time to be the form of government most vulnerable to direct corruption. I believe that Marxism is an ideology whose ultimate intentions are to pit the middle and lower classes against each other in order to ultimately seize power for themselves and their cause.

I will now make distinctions that will link Barack Obama with Marxist thought. In order to do that, I am going to take another direct quotation from Barack Obama's keynote speech (centered mostly around religion):

"After all, the problems of poverty and racism, the uninsured and the unemployed, are not simply technical problems in search of the perfect ten point plan. They are rooted in both societal indifference and individual callousness - in the imperfections of man.

Solving these problems will require changes in government policy, but it will also require changes in hearts and a change in minds. I believe in keeping guns out of our inner cities, and that our leaders must say so in the face of the gun manufacturers' lobby - but I also believe that when a gang-banger shoots indiscriminately into a crowd because he feels somebody disrespected him, we've got a moral problem. There's a hole in that young man's heart - a hole that the government alone cannot fix.

I believe in vigorous enforcement of our non-discrimination laws. But I also believe that a transformation of conscience and a genuine commitment to diversity on the part of the nation's CEOs could bring about quicker results than a battalion of lawyers. They have more lawyers than us anyway.

I think that we should put more of our tax dollars into educating poor girls and boys. I think that the work that Marian Wright Edelman has done all her life is absolutely how we should prioritize our resources in the wealthiest nation on earth. I also think that we should give them the information about contraception that can prevent unwanted pregnancies, lower abortion rates, and help assure that that every child is loved and cherished.

But, you know, my Bible tells me that if we train a child in the way he should go, when he is old he will not turn from it. So I think faith and guidance can help fortify a young woman's sense of self, a young man's sense of responsibility, and a sense of reverence that all young people should have for the act of sexual intimacy. I am not suggesting that every progressive suddenly latch on to religious terminology - that can be dangerous. Nothing is more transparent than inauthentic expressions of faith. As Jim has mentioned, some politicians come and clap -- off rhythm -- to the choir. We don't need that.

In fact, because I do not believe that religious people have a monopoly on morality, I would rather have someone who is grounded in morality and ethics, and who is also secular, affirm their morality and ethics and values without pretending that they're something they're not. They don't need to do that. None of us need to do that."
     -- Barack Obama

We'll start at the beginning. The problems he addresses that are hindering the American public are poverty and racism – both related directly to his voting base, the uninsured and the unemployed – two sectors he would like the government to control, and he laments on how these injustices of society are rooted in the 'imperfections of man.' I think what he really means is imperfection of the white man, but that's just my own speculation from hearing about his connections with Frank Marshall Davis, whom I will discuss in a moment. He purports that the solution to these problems of poverty, racism, the uninsured, and the unemployed can all be rectified through a change in government policy, i.e., socializing America. He believes in standing and shouting in a gun manufacturer's lobby, but believes the criminal aiming mercilessly into the crowd has a 'moral problem.' Let's talk about a moral problem Barack Obama: you will stand and scream at gun manufacturers but you will make excuses for the criminal that fires the gun and harms innocent victims whining that there is a 'hole in that young man's heart?' There is a hole in your head if you think that is the best solution to stopping gun violence. The benevolent attitude that Barack Obama bestows upon criminals just hawks me off. And what exactly does 'vigorous enforcement of our non-discrimination laws' mean? Our non-discrimination laws are enforced quite vigorously already. I don't mind non-discrimination laws because they ensure a more diverse, and ultimately more qualified field of applicants for a position, but extra enforcement of these laws is not necessary. The laws are in place, and most law-abiding citizens already know and understand all about them. He then goes on to demand that CEO's have a transformation of conscience and a genuine commitment to diversity. Note how much that statement mirrors Marxist thought that the 'ruling' class is oppressing the working class. Also, just an irritating bit of information I found while researching this speech. When he says "they have more lawyers than us anyway" when referencing the CEO's, he goes on in the next paragraph to talk about the work of Marian Wright Edelman – whom I researched and found out was a lawyer and the first African American woman admitted to the Mississippi state bar (Lewis). So I guess Barack knows just as many lawyers – especially since he is one (Novak). Just a warning to the elite lawyers in the Barack Obama Camp: Be ready to take any case you can make against this book to the Supreme Court. I will not stop until the Supreme Court reads the entirety of this book and then decides a verdict on my authority to utilize my First Amendment Rights to disclose these facts to those who choose to purchase this book. Ms. Edelman was also famous as an educator, activist, reformer, children's advocate and the founder and President of the Children's Defense Fund (Lewis). He then discusses tax dollars going to fund educating poor girls and boys, which is a nice sentiment, but it's rooted in more idealistic Marxist thought than the actual sentence alone can portray. But here is maybe the most disturbing yet revealing portion of Barack Obama's speech: "But, you know, my Bible tells me that if we train a child in the way he should go, when he is old he will not turn from it." So now I will discuss some of Barack Obama's influences in his formative years:

Frank Marshall Davis was a late Hawaiian Communist. "A careful reading of Obama's first memoir, 'Dreams From My Father,' reveals that his childhood mentor up to the age of 18 (a man he refers to only as Frank) was none other than the late communist Frank Marshall Davis, who fled Chicago after the FBI and Congress opened investigations into his 'subversive,' 'un-American activities.' In a belated story on the relationship, the Associated Press describes Davis as "left-leaning." In fact, Davis was a member of the Moscow-controlled Communist Party USA, according to the 153 report of the Commission on Subversive Activities of the Territory of Hawaii, which labeled him 'a bitter opponent of capitalism.' The report was introduced as evidence in the U.S. Senate Internal Security Subcommittee hearings probing the 'Scope of Soviet Activity in the United States.'

"Davis wrote militant poems as a black writer in Chicago, including one in which he hails the Soviet revolution: 'Smash on, victory-eating Red Army.' He also attacked traditional Christianity. As Obama was preparing to head off to college, he sat at Davis' feet in his Waikiki bungalow for bitter nightly bull sessions. Davis plied his impressionable guest with liberal shots of whiskey and advice, including: "Never Trust the white establishment. They'll train you so good, you'll start believing what they tell you about equal opportunity and the American way and all that sh**." He also said, "black people have a reason to hate."

In the memoir, Barack Obama says that he was "intrigued by old Frank, with his books and whiskey breath and the hint of hard-earned knowledge." He followed in Frank's footsteps as a community organizer for the socialist network in Chicago (IBD Editorials, Obama's Red Mentor).

COMMUNISM – THE RED DRAGON

I'm not using this textbook to define Communism, simply because it does not detail it in an accurate manner. I will be taking direct excerpts from Fredrick Engels document written in October-November of 1847 titled "The Principles of Communism."

"Communism is the doctrine of the conditions of the liberation of the proletariat. The proletariat is that class in society which lives entirely from the sale of its labor and does not draw profit from any kind of capital; whose weal and woe, whose life and death, whose sole existence depends on the demand for labor – hence, on the changing state of business, on the vagaries of unbridled competition. The proletariat, or the class of proletarians, is, in a word, the working class of the 19th century."

I'm not going to list all of the things I've already covered about Marxism up until this point, but this document goes on to detail the evolvement of the current proletariat in the Industrial Revolution – the creation of big factories who depend on low-skilled labor. And they state that the proletariat has not always existed. However, I believe this is a clever ploy by the Marxists to discourage the lower class of individuals into believing their circumstance is somewhat new and completely the fault of the Industrial Revolution. However, history states that lower classes of society have always existed, be they servants, peasants, etc. The "proletariat" as they define it may not have existed, but that is simply because they formed the word 'proletariat' in order to create a revolutionary movement.

This part sounds a little nonsensical to me so I'm going to quote it:

"Labor is a commodity, like any other, and its price is therefore determined by exactly the same laws that apply to other commodities. In a regime of big industry or of free competition – as we shall see, the two come to the same thing – the price of a commodity is, on the average, always equal to its cost of production. Hence, the price of labor is also equal to the cost of production of labor.

But, the costs of production of labor consist of precisely the quantity of means of subsistence necessary to enable the worker to continue working, and to prevent the working class from dying out. The worker will therefore get no more for his labor than is necessary for this purpose; the price of labor, or the wage, will, in other words, be the lowest, the minimum, required for the maintenance of life.

However, since business is sometimes better and sometimes worse, it follows that the worker sometimes gets more and sometimes gets less for his commodities. But, again, just as the industrialist, on the average of good times and bad, gets no more and no less for his commodities than what they cost, similarly on the average the worker gets no more and no less than his minimum.

This economic law of wages operates the more strictly the greater the degree to which big industry has taken possession of all branches of production."

Fredrick Engels asks the question *"What will this new social order have to be like?"*

"Above all, it will have to take the control of industry and of all branches of production out of the hands of mutually competing individuals, and instead institute a system in which all these branches of production are operated by society as a whole – that is, for the common account, according to a common plan, and with the participation of all members of society. It will, in other words, abolish competition and replace it with association.

Moreover, since the management of industry by individuals necessarily implies private property, and since competition is in reality merely the manner and form in which the control of industry by private property owners expresses itself, it follows that private property cannot be separated from competition and the individual management of industry. Private property must, therefore, be abolished and in its place must come the common utilization of all instruments of production and the distribution of all products according to common agreement – in a word, what is called the communal ownership of goods.

In fact, the abolition of private property is, doubtless, the shortest and most significant way to characterize the revolution in the whole social order which has been made necessary by the development of industry – and for this reason it is rightly advanced by communists as their main demand."

I'm physically sick because the next part of this document goes on to say that the Communists *"will establish a democratic constitution, and through this, the direct or indirect dominance of the proletariat."*

"Democracy would be wholly valueless to the proletariat if it were not immediately used as a means for putting through measures directed against private property and ensuring the livelihood of the proletariat. The main measures, emerging as the necessary result of existing relations, are the following:

(i) Limitation of private property through progressive taxation, heavy inheritance taxes, abolition of inheritance through collateral lines (brothers, nephews, etc.) forced loans, etc.

(ii) Gradual expropriation of landowners, industrialists, railroad magnates and shipowners, partly through competition by state industry, partly directly through compensation in the form of bonds.

(iii) Confiscation of the possessions of all emigrants and rebels against the majority of the people.

(iv) Organization of labor or employment of proletarians on publicly owned land, in factories and worships, with competition among the workers being abolished and with the factory owners, in so far as they still exist, being obliged to pay the same high wages as those paid by the state.

(v) An equal obligation on all members of society to work until such time as private property has been completely abolished. Formation of industrial armies, especially for agriculture.

(vi) Centralization of money and credit in the hands of the state through a national bank with state capital, and the suppression of all private banks and bankers.

(vii) Increase in the number of national factories, workshops, railroads, ships; bringing new lands into cultivation and improvement of land already under cultivation – all in proportion to the growth of the capital and labor force at the disposal of the nation.

(viii)   Education of all children, from the moment they can leave their mother's care, in national establishments at national cost. Education and production together.

(ix)   Construction, on public lands, of great palaces as communal dwellings for associate groups of citizens engaged in both industry and agriculture and combining in their way of life the advantages of urban and rural conditions while avoiding the one-sidedness and the drawbacks of each.

(x)   Destruction of all unhealthy and jerry-built dwellings in urban districts.

(xi)   Equal inheritance rights for children born in and out of wedlock.

(xii) Concentration of all means of transportation in the hands of the nation.

It is impossible, of course, to carry out all these measures at once. But one will always bring others in its wake. Once the first radical attack on private property has been launched, the proletariat will find itself forced to go ever further, to concentrate increasingly in the hands of the state all capital, all agriculture, all transport, all trade. All the foregoing measures are directed to this end; and they will become practicable and feasible, capable of producing their centralizing effects to precisely the degree that the proletariat, through its labor, multiplies the country's productive forces.

Finally, when all capital, all production, all exchange have been brought together in the hands of the nation, private property will disappear of its own accord, money will become superfluous, and production will so expand and man so change that society will be able to slough off whatever of its old economic habits may remain."

Let me give Communists a fair warning: if you authorize yourselves to trespass on my property in order to steal from or terrorize me, you will be shown why we have the Right to Bear Arms in the United States of America. Firearms and constant vigilance can protect private citizens when the government fails. Americans do not surrender without a fight.. Remember this Communists: You will not be given the opportunity to argue Communist ideology to me. You WILL be shot on sight. YOU WILL NOT take my property or my freedom as an American, and I will die in the effort to preserve it. This may seem like an overreaction, but if you thoroughly read the portion of the "Principles of Communism" authored by Fredrick Engel, you will understand that this is precisely what Communism will lead to. A seizure of private property by the 'new majority' – however, the 'new majority' does not give ample credit to their opposition, who are more than willing to die for the principles of freedom and liberty that Communism pretentiously and callously attempts to revoke.

Now that I have given that warning, I will go ahead and identify some of the most horrifying characteristics of this form of government. Note how Engels said that 'democracy would be wholly valueless to the proletariat if it were not immediately used as a means for putting through measures directed against private property and ensuring the livelihood of the proletariat.' What kind of adherence to the definition of democracy is this? This is why I dislike the term democracy from time to time. Democracy literally means 'for the good of the people' so power-hungry Communists figured out that the only way they could seize on the word is to convince the working class that they are the majority and that Communism purports to support that majority. It does not support the majority or any single individual. It supports the government seizing control of the people, and they use unrecognizable terms to many of the people that they claim to support to advocate this seizure. They want to keep the working class confused so they cannot fully understand that this form of government means COMPLETE control by the government over individuals.

This is just heinous: *"Limitation of private property through progressive taxation, heavy inheritance taxes, abolition of inheritance through collateral lines (brothers, nephews, etc.) forced loans, etc."* I hate Communism. I really do. Who the hell do these Communists think they are to demand that they have the authority to revoke citizens' right to private property? This means they will also revoke the proletariat's right to private property. NOTHING will be the property of a single individual because it will all be the property of the government. And what is this? WHAT is this? *"Equal inheritance rights for children born in and out of wedlock."* Did these jerks (I'm dulling it down) not just purport to eliminate inheritance altogether through taxes, but they would like to make provisions for children born out of wedlock? That makes absolutely no sense at all. NONE. The Communists would also like to create more industrialization and factories, which was previously asserted in this document to be the reason for the creation of the current working class.

How do they propose to abolish the proletariat while still creating more industrialization and factories? It doesn't add up, does it?

"An equal obligation on all members of society to work until such time as private property has been completely abolished. Formation of industrial armies, especially for agriculture." If people support this kind of nonsense, then this will be the downfall of the great country in which we live in. If you actually believe that you have the right to go onto anyone's private property and seize it, then you are not a true American and you do not abide by the Constitution and laws set forth by this country. But you can still have a positive outlook on life, Communists, for you can still move to China. Communism is brewing up over there quite nicely, so get the hell out of America and take this nonsense idea of Communism somewhere that it will be tolerated. Capitalists have nowhere else to go, and we will see that you never take this country over to Communism. NEVER. The United States of America is a Capitalist nation, and if you do not like that and would like to try a different form of government, then go to another country and try it. I'm sure you'll be back, but Stop polluting us with your negativity. We do not want you here. I am not supporting the idea that we cannot have oppositional views in this country; however, this form of government can never be productive to the extent that Capitalism has been for Americans, and Americans, specifically southerners and other conservative and liberal individuals, do not want Communism; therefore, if you do, then go to China or Russia – otherwise you sit there and be quiet and value everything that this Capitalistic form of government gives to you every single day.

My last specific quotation from that excerpt will be this:

"Centralization of money and credit in the hands of the state through a national bank with state capital, and the suppression of all private banks and bankers."

Americans, it is time to think. Think hard. If you're bordering on supporting Barack Obama and his form of Marxism, which will eventually lead to this, then think. Right now. Do you want the federal government to control all of the money in this country? They've done a pretty poor job controlling the small portion of it that they do have up until this point. But this is fundamental. People have got to understand that the government is an institution of political insurrection and

corruption. "Power corrupts, but absolute power corrupts absolutely."
– Lord John Emerich Edward Dalberg Acton, historian and moralist.

Barack Obama's link to the Communist movement: I have now been informed by Mark Levin that Barack Obama has been putting forth provisions to monitor the free and fair votes of those citizens employed by the government in Unions. This is one of the most staunch injustices I have seen come out of the Barack Obama camp so far. YOU have no authority to monitor union voters, Barack Obama, nor has anything like this happened in the history of free and fair voting elections in the United States of America. You want to log the members down in your memory that opposed your nomination so you can target them or ensure that they lose their jobs in the future. You are a despicable person and you act as though Americans serve only the purpose of furthering your cause, Barack Obama. We don't. We serve to further America's cause.

My source for this information is the Mark Levin Show, various conservative blogs, and an article published by Newser. The article is titled "Nev. Union Bullied Voters, Clinton Claimed." This article states the following: "Bill Clinton said today he personally witnessed reps from the pro-Obama Culinary Workers union threaten members who vowed to vote for Hillary in the Nevada caucuses. Workers who weren't pro-Obama would have their schedules changed to keep them from voting, Clinton claimed. "This is ludicrous," the union's political director told Politico, noting that workers can take time off to vote without consulting the union. Last night, Bill said he and Chelsea were mobbed by workers promising to buck the union's endorsement and vote for Hillary. Bill says he personally saw a representative threaten each of them. He told the Huffington Post today that his wife had been 'flooded' with complaints of similar abuses. Obama's campaign challenged the Clintons to file a formal complaint about the incidents."

Remember that the mainstream media will not report on things like this. How would they ever justify it? They could not. We cannot ignore every piece of information that is not directly reported on by the mainstream media. This is crucial information, and in the blog I read on this topic, the Hillary Clinton campaign had gotten numerous complaints of coercion from members of unions claiming that Barack Obama was making subtle threats to them if they did not vote for him. It comes down to whether you believe Hillary Clinton or Barack Obama, I suppose. I would really like to believe that this is not factual;

however, I believe that it is much more factual than the mainstream media will ever let on to. But I have disclosed to you that I have no 'credible' source for this information so you will have to take it with a grain of salt. However, Barack Obama, if this is factual, it is in your best interest to never make such a threat again because this injustice will not be tolerated by the American public.

Barack Obama also seeks to eliminate the United States' supply of nuclear weapons. An idiot of epic proportions is what we're dealing with here. Really, there is no other way to describe the man at this juncture; he has absolutely no credibility, foresight, or understanding of the global position of the United States of America. What would even momentarily convince Americans to disassemble our nuclear weapons programs when Iran has been building their weapons arsenal ? They do not have the technology that we have to date, but there is absolutely no logical reason to disassemble our nuclear weapons programs because, in doing so, we would be diminishing our own national security in the wake of terrorist attacks that occurred less than 1 full decade ago!

Barack Obama, you will be the downfall of America if you have your way as President. Obama believes that "the United States should greatly reduce its stockpiles [of nuclear weapons] to lower the threat of nuclear terrorism, aides say." Barack Obama has no problem leaving America wide open to foreign invasion. I wonder why. When will people see that Obama has no stake in the national security of the United States of America? Again I will point out that he voted against a foreign intelligence surveillance act but for a modification and extension of the Patriot Act. What kind of stance does that indicate regarding the security of the United States of America? We will be spending our tax money funding a $1 Trillion dollar World Poverty Act (introduced by Senator Obama), but Senator does not see the use in providing necessary foreign intelligence surveillance? What is this nonsense? Barack Obama has no authority to monitor United States citizens via the Patriot Act when it is clear that he is not doing it to quell terrorism. If the man wanted to alleviate terrorism, he would be approaching this completely differently. Barack Obama has a way of hand-holding the corrupt while demonizing those with strong morals and convictions. Where was Barack Obama on September 11, 2001? I want to know! I want to know if he remembers what devastation and peril feel and look like in the United States of America; and I wonder if he savored the peril or if he was repulsed by it.

Fascism/Totalitarianism

Barack Obama has fascist tendencies but cannot be defined as a full-fledged Fascist. Fascists are individuals disenchanted with the liberal mindset valuing the individual and disenchanted by the socialist ideals of contending classes. Fascists believe in a perception of the world as an all-encompassing whole. Barack Obama is not disenchanted with socialism, but he is entranced by the idea of 'a mighty empire under the control of a single party and a supreme leader.' (Ball p. 177) He believes that his ivy-league education has bestowed upon him great insight that lowly Americans cannot even pretend to understand. He is focused primarily, and without regard to any other pressing matter, on the 'socialist emphasis on contending social classes,' whom he would really like to pit against each other so he can seize complete control of this country. This is about control and power for Barack Obama. He is so close to it that he can taste it, and he will not stop revoking rights he believes he has the authority to revoke along the way. I can tell just by hearing Barack Obama speak that he is now consumed by the idea of ultimate power. You can hear it in his voice, the way he stutters when he is talking about anything other than his ideas to stifle the economy and simultaneously elevate the United States Government. The want for power is resonating from Barack Obama right now, and a lot of people can hear it. Some can't. But not everyone can be convinced. I've spent a lot of time trying to convince people of views and they simply cannot or will not hear or understand my standpoint, but this is human nature. Humans fight with one another. I hope to convince quite a few people that read this book to reconsider voting for Barack Obama, but I know that I cannot convince them all, nor do I propose to. However, these facts I am presenting are important information to the freedom and stability of the American public, and I know that those words and the facts I put behind them, will at least make people second guess the benevolence of the all-mighty Barack Obama.

Totalitarianism attempts to seize control of an entire society – its government, and all other social, political, cultural, and economic institutions. Totalitarianism is a very oppressive form of government if that's not already evident. It is a form of government centered upon control over individuals by a single person or a small group of leaders.

STALINISM

Three features distinguish Stalinism from Marxism-Leninism: Lenin believed in the working class's state of false consciousness, but Stalin believed that the party itself was corrupt and needed a single all-wise, all-knowing leader to facilitate the movement. The 'cult of personality' was formed around Stalin under this premise. Stalinism adheres to the notion of socialism in a single country. Marx and Engels disagreed with this and thought that this was a more universal concept that could be utilized by many countries. Stalin believed in a theory known as dialectical materialism, which Marx and Engels never used. Dialectical materialism refers to the idea that there are no accidents and that everything happens because it is supposed to. "All is determined by the movement of matter."

I've listened to Mark Levin call Barack Obama a Stalinist at times, and I understand why, but he does not fit all of the criteria necessary to be labeled a full-fledged Stalinist. Barack Obama believes himself to be the sole vanguard of the movement, the single, all-wise, all-knowing genius; however, he does not believe that his views of socialism should be restricted only to this country. Hence why he speaks of Europeans so fondly and spent so much time with them on his trip to the Middle East (Erlanger). He is a Marxist in that he believes his form of socialism to be a universal concept that can be accepted by people of all faiths, creeds, or nationalities. I also have never heard him reference anything that could be referred to as 'dialectical materialism.' Just because I have never witnessed it does not mean he hasn't said it, but I'm not going to make an argument for it since I have no evidence to put behind it. But there is another similarity between Barack Obama and Stalin; Barack Obama also seeks to 'eliminate not only potential political opponents but theoretical or ideological critics as well.' Hence why he refuses to have an official Presidential Political Debate, and will not allow any opponent to criticize his views or opinions without whining about oppression or claiming racism or some other form of foul play. It is very difficult for ideologues to have a full on debate about issues because the notion of some ideologies can stifle productive thoughts on solutions. Marxist thought, I believe, is particularly subject to a complete denouncement of any alternative notions to the ideology, and Marxists are not fond of those who criticize their thoughts and ideals on the 'utopian' society they ultimately hope to create.

ECOLOGY

I will not be delving deep into "Green" politics because I am not interested in this political ideology, and I found it extremely boring and listless when I studied it. However, it is important to note a few things about Ecology as an Ideology. Mostly because the current Speaker of the House, Nancy Pelosi, who is currently on a five week paid vacation, is an environmentalist – or ecologist – to the worst extreme.

An environmental crisis is really the sole issue of this movement. There have been a series of crises dealing with ecological and environmental decay that ecology seeks to eliminate or quell. This ideology is concerned with nature – preserving wildlife, especially animals nearing extinction; preserving forests (however, it should be noted that forests need to be trimmed back in order to prevent forest fires), preserving natural ecosystems. They are also concerned with a term known as the greenhouse effect – the warming of the earth's atmosphere. Ecologists have also recently been entranced by the notion of global warming. Global warming as an environmental deterrent has already been disproven. I really don't feel like wasting the time in this book refuting the tenants of global warming, but it has been noted that the changes in the environment are due to factors mostly out of the control of humans. It is clear through historical study that the climate has gone through multiple changes throughout eras so it is not unreasonable to assume that we are going through a small climate change right now. But this will not affect the day-to-day lives of humans because we can adapt to any climate change that occurs, unless another Ice Age occurs. If you are unconvinced by my explanation, go to globalwarminghoax.com for a more comprehensive overview of why this myth is false.

Ecologists believe that these problems are 'interconnected' and directly involve human participation – which they think should be immediately reformed to meet the needs of the environment. The Ball/ Dagger textbook cites the internal combustion engine as one of the innovative by-products that has caused damage to the environment. Ecologists deplore the idea that humans are above animals and nature; they support (and I support to some extent) the notion that humans and animals should live in cooperation with each other and respect one another. This is where Ecology gets ideological. Ecologists believe that human beings have an obligation to care for the environment (including nature and animals) because we have the ability to do so. Ecology seeks to provide a more hopeful view of human interaction with plants, animals, and Mother Nature. (Ball p.241)

I do not necessarily disagree with all of the ideals of this ideological standpoint because I do believe that humans should respect nature and animals, but I disagree with the lengths that some politicians will take these beliefs. Humans have the capacity for rational, individual, and articulate thought. Animals, unfortunately, cannot convey their thoughts to us, but we assume that since we can speak and communicate with one another that we are the ones in control of society. Humans must ensure that society continues on, but I do not agree with staunch environmental policies that will sky-rocket prices and ridiculously increase taxes. There is a level of preservation that is necessary, but we must not allow these ideals to cloud our judgment when looking at other – more pertinent issues.

CAPITALISM

This textbook doesn't have a chapter on Capitalism – as I stated before, the book is written from a Pro-Marxist standpoint – however, I don't need that text to give a concise overview of Capitalism. I will be referencing a textbook titled "Economics" by Paul Krugman and Robin Wells. I will be discussing the definition of Economics in the context of Capitalism, supply and demand, also the elasticity and inelasticity of goods, individual's relationship to the market, trade-offs, market efficiency, international trade, and taxes. These principles are critical to understanding the way in which a Capitalist economy is the most beneficial form of government for the individual citizen.

AMERICAN ECONOMY OVERVIEW

The American Economy is a large, productive, and efficient network of concepts and theories that have been centered on Capitalistic principles and the free market. Controls and limitations can be placed on the economy by federal and state governments, which makes the American economy technically a 'mixed economy,' but the founding fathers had clear capitalistic intentions for this country. Capitalism allows the individual the freedom to any business venture or idea that he or she has; however, these personal businesses will be privately funded and operated. This is one of the main reasons that a capitalist must understand the business climate and economy of their country – because it is up to the individual to make their own business attempts or to take the opportunities granted to them by other small and privately-owned businesses. Capitalism also allows for the individual to own private property that he or she can claim as his/her own. The individual works and specializes for monetary compensation that they will be able to have the freedom to choose how to spend. If an individual is granted $1,000 for performing a job for three weeks, he or she has the discretion to spend that money (aside from the taxes taken by the federal government which theoretically, in a Capitalist society, should be as low as possible) on whatever they choose to be their immediate want or need at the time. This could include so many things – we could spend quite a while thinking of them all. However, it is more important to note the freedom of the individual to spend the money he/she earns how he/she deems it should be spent. The role of the federal government is to regulate mismanagement of businesses mostly. The federal government should ultimately be instituting policies that will stimulate positive growth for the economy, not pouring more money into the federal government so they can control, and in the long run, extremely denigrate the efficiency of the industry. I would like for people to recall a local bureaucracy or union whose workers are motivated and given incentives to complete their jobs effectively. Bureaucracies and unions are compensated well above the minimum wage, but the effectiveness of these industries is questioned from time to time. There is no doubt that the laborers are always present to do their jobs and are properly compensated to perform those jobs; however, the workers seem to find the job dull;

they do not seem motivated to do their job because they enjoy it. They seem motivated by the federal funds bestowed upon them to complete the job. I value the labor of these individuals, but I wonder if they would ultimately be more satisfied with their careers if they would seek a job more aligned with their specific interests. I could be wrong, and maybe these individuals really are happy with their jobs, and if so, then you should keep that job. That's why the government has created jobs because some of them are relevant, efficient, and extremely productive for this country. However, if you are one of those people that are not motivated to do their government-sponsored job, then look for something else. Just check out your other possibilities and see if maybe you can find something that will be more suitable to you and will, in the long run, make you a much happier and efficient worker.

"An economy succeeds to the extent that it, literally, delivers the goods." (p.2)

Economists study trends in the economy in the form of statistical or numerical values to find out the 'extent that it...delivers the goods.' An economy succeeds when the benefits of production outweigh the costs. That is to say, the revenue that privately owned businesses constituting the American economy take in collectively must outweigh the cost that the businesses and economy incurs by undertaking the business ventures. So the businesses must profit for the economy to flourish and continue to efficiently deliver goods. And, in the United States of America, individuals make decisions as to the goods and services that will be produced and consumed in the country. "A market economy is an economy in which decisions about production and consumption are made by individual producers and consumers." This is an important portion of the economy that differentiates it from the ideology of Marxism. Marxism/Communism purports that the government should control what is produced and consumed by the public, whereas, in a Capitalist economy, the individual has the right to choose.

"The invisible hand refers to the 'way a market economy manages to harness the power of self-interest for the good of society.'" (p.3)

"Market failure is when instead of promoting the interests of society as a whole, the individual's attempts actually make society worse off. The good news...is that economic analysis can be used to diagnose cases of market failure." (p.3)

Market failure or the failure of a specific business is inevitable because not every business can succeed. The success of the business depends on the individual's attempts to facilitate the development of a product that some portion of the American public will find useful and will, therefore, make a priority to purchase. If the entrepreneur can develop such a product, then his/her business venture will succeed. But it is irrational to think it is a flaw of the economy that every idea cannot succeed in creating mass sums of wealth for the individual. It is an arduous task to design such a product, market it, advertise it, produce it (cost effectively), distribute it, because then, and only then after the distribution of the product to the public can an entrepreneur reap the benefits of his/her investment. It is important to note: "Such troubled periods are a regular feature of modern economies. The act is that the economy does not always run smoothly: it experiences fluctuations, a series of ups and downs. By middle age, a typical American will have experienced three or four downs, known as recessions. During a severe recession, millions of workers may be laid off. Like market failure, recessions are a fact of life: but also like market failure, they are a problem to which economic analysis offers some solutions. Recessions are one of the main concerns of the branch of economics known as macroeconomics." (p.4)

This is what I'm talking about when I refer to Karl Marx not accounting for the fact that we have dedicated an entire branch of economic study to alleviating recessions and depressions in this country. It is not a perfect branch of science, but there is no perfect branch of science, and it is extremely beneficial to the capitalist economy in rectifying major economic concerns or crises.

"At the beginning of the twentieth century, most Americans lived under conditions that we would now think of as extreme poverty. Only 10 percent of homes had flush toilets, only 8 percent had central heating, only 2 percent had electricity, and almost nobody had a car, let alone a washing machine or air conditioning Such comparisons are a stark reminder of how much our lives have been changed by economic growth, the growing ability of the economy to produce goods and services." (p.4)

^I think this is a very good example of what the productivity of a Capitalist economy can yield.

A couple of definitions that are important to understanding the American economy:

• "The real cost of an item is its opportunity cost: what you must give up in order to get it." (p.7) You weigh the opportunity cost of your items everyday, perhaps without even realizing it. Whatever you must forego in order to obtain something else is the opportunity cost of the item. This theory can apply to many facets of your life.

• "You make a trade-off when you compare the costs with the benefits of doing something." (p.8) Comparing the costs and benefits of your options usually enables the consumer to make a more educated, efficient choice. Not always, by any means, as it is completely up to personal desire, tastes, and preferences what an individual will choose.

• "An incentive is anything that offers rewards to people who change their behavior." (p.9) I go on and on about incentive because I love the concept of it. I think incentive has molded Americans into a group of humans that looks to exceed expectations rather than being stagnant and complacent at the hands of the government.

• "Interaction of choices – my choices affect your choices, and vice versa – is a feature of most economic situations. The results of this interaction are often quite different from what the individuals intend." (p.11)

Another important aspect of the economy: "In a market economy, individuals engage in trade: They provide goods and services to others and receive goods and services in return. There are gains from trade: people can get more of what they want through trade than they could if they tried to be self-sufficient. This increase in output is due to specialization: each person specializes in the task that he or she is good at performing. (p.12)

MARKET EQUILIBRIUM AND EFFICIENCY

Important definitions concerning efficiency and equilibrium (from the textbook I quoted earlier, most of this information comes directly from that text):

•An economic situation is in equilibrium when no individual would be better off doing something different. (p.13)"

•An economy is efficient if it takes all opportunities to make some people better off without make other people worse off. (p.14)

•Equity means that everyone gets his or her fair share. Since people can disagree about what's "fair," equity isn't as well-defined concept as efficiency. (p.15)

•A competitive market is a market in which there are many buyers and sellers of the same good or service.

"Everyone has to make choices about what to do and what not to do. Individual choice is the basis of economics – if it doesn't involve choice, it isn't economics. The reason that choices must be made are because resources – anything that can be used to produce something else – are scarce." (p.17)

To understand a competitive market economy, we must discuss the supply and demand model in detail. "There are five key elements in this model: 1) the demand curve, 2) the supply curve, 3) the set of factors that cause the demand curve to shift, and the set of factors that cause the supply curve to shift, 4) the equilibrium price, 5) The way the equilibrium price changes when the supply or demand curves shift. (pp.56-105)

1) Demand and the demand curve: The law of demand says that a higher price for a good, other things equal, leads people to demand a smaller quantity of the good. A demand curve is a graphical representation of the demand schedule. It shows how much of a good or service consumers want to buy at any given price. The quantity demanded is the actual amount consumers are willing to buy at some specific price.

2) Supply and the supply curve: The quantity supplied is the actual amount of a good or service people are willing to sell at some specific price. A supply schedule shows how much of a good or service would be supplied at different prices. And a supply curve shows graphically how much of a good or service people are willing to sell at any given price.

3) Factors that cause the demand and supply curves to shift: Changes in the prices of related goods, changes in income, changes in tastes, and changes in expectations

4) An explanation of equilibrium price: A competitive market is in equilibrium when price has moved to a level at which the quantity demanded of a good equals the quantity supplied of that good. The price at which this takes place is the equilibrium price, also referred to as the market-clearing price. The quantity of the good bought and sold at that price is the equilibrium quantity. It is the price that "clears the market" by ensuring that every buyer willing to pay that price finds a seller willing to sell at that price, and vice versa.

5) The effect of supply/demand curve shifts on the equilibrium price: An explanation for why the market price of a good falls if it is above the equilibrium price: There is a surplus of a good when the quantity supplied exceeds the quantity demanded. Surpluses occur when the price is above its equilibrium level. An explanation of why the market price rises if it is below the equilibrium price: There is a shortage of a good when the quantity demanded exceeds the quantity supplied. Shortages occur when the price is below its equilibrium level.

Supply and demand models must be closely scrutinized in order to understand business trends including productivity, the impact of the goods and services produced in the economy, and it can also predict future changes in supply or demand based on the principles and laws of supply and demand respectively.

PRICE CEILINGS/FLOORS AND THE MINIMUM WAGE

"Price controls are legal restrictions on how high or low a market price may go. They can take two forms: a price ceiling, a maximum price sellers are allowed to charge for a good, or a price floor, a minimum price buyers are required to pay for a good." (p.84)

Price controls are implemented into a Capitalist economy in 2 main ways (it is not limited to these ways, but these are two prime examples): the minimum wage is a common price floor, and a maximum price that a business can charge for their product is a typical price ceiling.

"A market or an economy is inefficient if there are missed opportunities: some people could be made better off without making other people worse off." (p.86)

Price ceilings and floors typically lead to market inefficiency because some people could be made better off without making other people worse off. Price floors cause inefficiency in the 'allocation of sales among sellers,' 'wasted resources,' and 'inefficiently high quality.' For further clarification: there are individuals that would buy goods for less money or businesses could employ more qualified individuals for less money than they are being forced to charge or pay to other individuals. There are wasted resources – surplus production, wasted time and effort. "Consider the minimum wage. Would-be workers who spend many hours searching for jobs, or waiting in line in the hope of getting jobs, play the same role in the case of price floors as hapless families searching for apartments in the case of price ceilings." Those are all wasted resources to the American economy because the economy values the production and work of the individual to meet the demand but not over-exceed demand in this country. And, "(a)gain like price ceilings, price floors lead to inefficiency in the quality of good produced." (pp.86-94)

Another explanation of this effect: "Price ceilings typically lead to inefficiency in the form of wasted resources: people spend money and expend effort in order to deal with the shortages caused by the price ceiling. Price ceilings often lead to inefficiency in that the goods being offered are of inefficiently low quality: sellers offer low-quality goods at a low price even though buyers would prefer a higher quality at a higher price. A black market is a market in which goods or services are bought and sold illegally – either because it is illegal to sell them at all or because the prices charged are legally prohibited by a price ceiling.

The minimum wage is a legal floor to the wage rate, which is the market price of labor.

One last example of price floor and ceiling inefficiency: Price floors lead to inefficient allocation of sales among sellers: those who would be willing to sell the good at the lowest price are not always those who actually manage to sell it. Price floors often lead to inefficiency in that goods of inefficiently high quality are offered: sellers offer high-quality goods at a high price, even though buyers would prefer a lower quality at a lower price.

ELASTICITY

The definition of elasticity is a measure of responsiveness to changes in price of incomes. The price elasticity of demand is a measure of the responsiveness of the quantity demanded to price. The price elasticity of supply measures the responsiveness of the quantity supplied to price.

The price elasticity of demand = % change in quantity demanded % change in price

"The larger the price elasticity of demand, the more responsive the quantity demanded is to price. When the price elasticity of demand is large – when consumers change their quantity demanded by a large percentage compared with the percent change in the price – economists say that demand is highly elastic." (p.110-111)

"Demand is elastic if the price elasticity of demand is greater than 1, inelastic if the price elasticity of demand is less than 1, and unit-elastic if the price elasticity of demand is exactly 1." (p.114) An elastic good means that with a shift in price, there will be a significant change in quantity demanded. An inelastic good means that with a shift in price, there will not or cannot be a change in quantity demanded. Elasticity measures the necessity of a good in the economy as a whole – and the measurement usually pertains to people's everyday lives and costs they will incur. If there is a 'price effect' on the product, then after a price increase, each unit sold sells at a higher price, which tends to raise revenue. If there is a 'quantity effect,' after a price increase fewer units are sold, which tends to lower revenue. (p.117) Theoretically both of these situations are possible when considering price elasticity. However, it is important to note in this general election that price elasticity is a major factor in why it is critical for America to drill for oil. There is no way around it. The past few months have shown that a 'quantity effect' is occurring as gas prices rise higher and higher. If we do not drill for oil and create a sufficient supply of crude oil for the United States of America, then the economy will fail over time. That is my projection.

TAXES

"Tax policy always has two goals. On the one hand, governments strive to achieve tax efficiency: they try to minimalize the direct and indirect costs to the economy of tax collection. On the other hand, governments also seek tax fairness, or tax equity: they try to ensure that the "right" people actually bear the burden of taxes. The central dilemma in tax policy – the dilemma that led to London's poll tax riot – is that an efficient tax may not seem fair, and a seemingly fair tax may not be efficient. So there is a fundamental trade-off between equity and efficiency." (p.494)

"A tax system causes deadweight losses because taxes distort incentives: the incentives at the margin for producers to produce and consumers to consumers are different from what they would have been without the tax, so people change their behavior. As a result, the tax that distorts incentives the last also minimizes any deadweight losses. So if the goal, in choosing whom to tax, is to minimize deadweight loss, then taxes should be imposed on those who have the most inelastic response – people who will change their behavior the last in response to he tax. (Unless they have a tendency of riot, of course.)(p.495)

"In considering the efficiency of a tax, we must also take into account administrative costs of the tax: the resources actually used both to collect the tax and to pay it. The most familiar administrative cost of the U.S. tax system is the time individuals spend filling out their tax forms or the money they spend on accountants to do their taxes for them. (The costs of operating the Internal Revenue Service are actually quite small by comparison.)(p.495)

These quotations are all very important to understanding the incentives and drawbacks of implementing taxes on the American Economy. Taxes are not to be taken lightly in a Capitalist economy because they can have severe negative impacts on the economy if not closely analyzed and scrutinized before being implemented.

LIBERALISM

I love this first quote in the Ball/Dagger textbook on Liberalism: "Over himself, over his own body and mind, the individual is sovereign." – John Stuart Mill (p.43)

This is the reason that I ultimately know that even true liberals will not consent to a Barack Obama regime. Liberalism is centered around the concept of promoting individual liberty. There are two distinct branches of this ideology that rival somewhat in their beliefs on how to utilize the concept of individual liberty. These ideologies are 'neoclassical liberalism' and 'welfare liberalism' – which will both be discussed in detail later in this section. I do have quite a bit of respect for the neoclassical liberal movement and could be considered one of sorts. I don't necessarily subscribe to a particular party, but I have found that a few different ideologies generally mirror my viewpoint: individualist conservative, libertarian, and neoclassical liberal. I will explain the relation between the three in a moment, but do note that liberalism and conservatism are linked together and can usually feed positively off of one another to promote the greater overall good of society. That is what we strive for in this country. "The words liberal and liberty both derive from the Latin liber, meaning 'free.'" (p.43)

Liberals generally conceive of human beings as rational individuals capable of logical thought and capable of understanding the concept of personal responsibility -- the responsibility of an individual to weigh the consequences of one's actions. Humans, liberals believe, are a competent breed of human and should be given the freedom to pursue their own interests and goals. Liberals believe that humans have self-control and can usually suppress their passions and desires when necessary. (p.44)

I must point this out before we get too far into a discussion of liberalism, and this seems the appropriate place to interject that Barack Obama is not a liberal. I really do not care what he calls himself or what people have convinced themselves that he is, but, he is NOT a liberal. Liberal thought is grounded in the freedom of the individual to make choices and decisions for themselves. Barack Obama believes that he can make those decisions for the American public regardless of what we have to say about it. Also, please note how contrary to Marxist thought on human nature that Liberalism is. Liberals believe in human nature and that those principles affect the way that humans interact and all that jazz. Those ideas are not characteristic of Marxist thought, which proposes that people are social or communal creatures. Marxism also supports the idea that individuals are simply too ignorant or brainwashed by the circumstance the 'ruling' or middle class has apportioned them by no fault of their own, to understand their own lives. Liberalism gives a much more positive outlook on human nature than Marxism or Communism. And that's why I have a little bit of a soft spot for it. I like the idea of individuals being free of oppression, free of the government, free of government restrictions, but mostly, free to make his/her own decisions. I understand that some liberals are drawn to the open-ness of Barack Obama to all people; however, I do not believe that the liberals intending to vote for Obama really understand the extent to which he will revoke their freedoms without regard after he gets their vote. Liberals really must understand that Liberalism, in essence, and specifically in reference to neoclassical liberalism, is the opposite of Marxism. The Kryptonite of Marxism, so to speak. This ideology is so cemented in logic and grounded in reality that it apportions freedom and responsibility to the individual. These ideas are a threat to Marxism/Communism and anyone who purports to support either of those ideologies. That is why they largely have given up fighting it and have taken a more passive aggressive role to addressing those they deem to be liberal. Books could be and have been written on the clarity and precise nature of the ideology of Liberalism; however, I will spend only a short period explaining the similarities and vast distinctions between neoclassical and welfare liberalism.

NEOCLASSICAL LIBERALISM

Now that I'm using this Ball/Dagger textbook as a reference to write my own book, I'm becoming increasingly annoyed by how short the passages on Capitalism and Neoclassical Liberalism are and how poorly they are explained. I'm glad I want to extrapolate and draw my own conclusions because this book is of little to no help in giving me evidence that supports the argument I am trying to make; however, logic usually prevails so I've still been able to manage. I had cited a few quotes directly from the textbook, but I decided to remove those in light of the copyright law and just give my own description of neoclassical liberalism. Trust me, I understand it better than these authors do anyway, they had less than one full page on this ideology.

But first, neoclassical or classical liberals advocate a very limited federal government that intends to protect the people and facilitate the growth of the economy. Neoclassical liberals believe the duty of the government is more to stand guard over the citizens who should be able to utilize the freedoms and liberties granted to them by their state and the Constitution of the United States. Neoclassical liberalism is fairly and justly related to libertarianism on ideological grounds. Libertarianism is considered by many political scientists to be the most consistent of all modern ideologies because it advocates the government be limited in the social and economic sectors. For more clarification: welfare liberals advocate government intervention in the economic sector, while socially conservative individuals advocate government intervention in the social sector. Libertarianism does not advocate the absence of government, as some critics will attempt to link the ideology with anarchism; however, libertarianism advocates a very limited government in all facets including peoples' public lives and their private lives. Libertarians believe that government restrictions of any kind can only lead to mismanagement and stagnancy since people should have the free will to make the choices they desire – given that they do not cause imminent harm or danger to anyone else. I believe that libertarianism is the 'free-ist' of ideologies, in that it values the freedom of the individual to make choices for their own life ALWAYS over government intervention. This can be taken to an unproductive or dangerous extent in some cases, but the ideology supports the notion that the individual is responsible for his/her own actions and can handle the consequences of those actions. The consistency of this ideology should be noted as an attribute because it does not purport to control the people in any way. Libertarians believe that people should be free of control by the government all together. And libertarians are also big on national security, but most, not all, libertarians I have found do not support the Patriot Act for Constitutional reasons that I understand; however, I did support the Patriot Act when it was introduced into legislation by George W. Bush because I believed it to be of vital importance to national security at the time. But times are changing, and I am starting to revoke my faith in the Patriot Act to only be utilized for the good of this country and not for unjust and un-Constitutional purposes.

Neoclassical or classical liberals also stress the 'importance of individual property rights, natural rights, the need for constitutional limitations on government, and, especially, freedom of the individual from any kind of external restraint.' The Enlightenment period was instrumental in the development of this ideological process because this era promoted the idea of liberty fought for in the American and French revolutions. Adam Smith, the renowned Capitalistic author and scholar, is an example of a classical liberal. John Stuart Mill is another example. Adam Smith introduced many interesting ideological and economic thoughts concerning laissez-faire economics and the prosperity of a capitalist nation.

Neoclassical liberals adhere to a representative government governed by the people, for the people. They do not believe that matter directly influencing an individual's life should be left for the government to decide; neoclassical liberals believe that people should be involved in making their own decisions because of their conception of humankind and human nature. This line of thought focuses upon the rationality of individuals to make decisions most suitable for their own life, and the idea is that when people make decisions for themselves to make their own life and the life of those they care for better, that they will make the whole of society better off in the long run. Adam Smith contended that these individual decisions are not intentionally interconnected by individuals in society, but intelligent and thought-based decisions on an individual's life can positively affect other people in the economy as well. This has proven to be true over time, as the growing prosperity of one industry may sponsor growth of another related industry. This occurs when a good has a complement – a good that 'complements' the first good. An example of a complement would be a hot dog bun to a hot dog. If the hot dog industry makes improvements to their industry and can produce more hotdogs for the American public to consume, then the manufacturer of hotdog buns must keep up with the pace of the hotdog business in order to meet demand. The opposite of a complement in a capitalist society is a substitute. A substitute is a good that can be substituted for a similar, less-expensive model of basically the same product. These industries can be encouraged to innovate by the evolvement and prosperity of another related industry because that industry must be able to compete to maintain its place in the market. Two different hotdog manufacturers would be defined as substitutes. These theories prove that competition between industries enhances innovative technology and progressive advancement in industries. This concept of individuals' aiding one-another unintentionally can be found in many other facets of life; I have only explained it in the context of economics.

Inequalities between wealth and power, between class systems and the Industrial Revolution propelled idealists to find an alternative solution to this ideological standpoint; hence comes Marxism, socialism, and welfare liberalism to dispute the tenants of this ideology.

WELFARE LIBERALISM

Welfare liberals believe, to some extent, in the concept of individual liberty and freedom. However, the difference comes when welfare liberals attempt to maintain government programs in order to facilitate equality in the marketplace and outside of it. Welfare liberals believe that government can be utilized positively to promote the freedom of the less-fortunate members of society. (p.70)

Since welfare liberalism supports sectors of government control, it cannot be free of political corruption for the sake of power. That's another reason I like libertarianism and neoclassical liberalism. Both ideologies advocate very little government and, in essence, forego any power struggle between politicians on how much the government should control the American public.

T.H. Green contended that the essence of liberalism is the desire to remove obstacles that inhibit the positive growth of society. Welfare liberalism is centered around a notion that the practices within a society that impede desired equality should be repealed, prohibited, and corrected. However, in order to accomplish these tasks, they implement policies and procedures contrary to Capitalistic thought. Some of these laws, such as non-discrimination laws, are essential to a free and functioning society; however, many of these policies are not so critical and actually inhibit productivity by depleting the idea of incentive rather than promoting it. (p.70)

Welfare liberals are slightly obsessed with themselves and their ever-benevolent intentions to create more government programs in order to facilitate 'equality.' The authors of the Ball/Dagger textbook have now seriously annoyed me because they do not accurately explain neoclassical liberalism, and afterwards, they proceed to justify welfare liberalism by pointing out that our 'higher' selves desire some form of government control over the individual – and, for the first time in the book, the authors identify themselves with a particular ideology. Welfare liberalism purports to address and challenge systematic problems in the marketplace that inhibit the growth and productivity of the society; however, this is where liberals allow themselves to linger dangerously close to socialism/Marxism/and Communism. They allow these principles of desired equality to cloud their judgment about the uninhibited freedom of the individual. They claim that freedom can only be truly achieved if individuals are leveled by the government to be equal in the marketplace. I believe that this line of thought is not consistent with the logical tenants of freedom and it should be noted that when the government attempts to vainly alleviate 'poverty and illness, prejudice and ignorance' it rarely, if ever, actually succeeds in finding productive solutions that will eliminate these things and not simply exacerbate them to create more prejudice and poverty. Welfare liberals dismiss the idea of economic responsibility by the individual and asserts that individuals should be apportioned a level of income or job stability by the government. However, these policies rarely if ever yield the desired result, and usually just result in continued economic stagnancy.

An adherent to welfare liberalist thought: 'Society, acting through government, should establish public schools and hospitals' (p.71) because that has worked out so well up until this point. The public school system in this country is floundering and needs more funding to satisfy the teachers and the immediate scholarly needs of the students. However, these schools are not properly funded, and they do not have the authority to institute rules and regulations for their students without the fear that the federal government will step in and label them corrupt for punishing children or authoritarian for trying to implement ideals into school systems that parents may not fully agree with. This is just detrimental to the positive development of children because children need to learn a few basic, core principles in the schooling process, and those are discipline, dedication, and respect for authority. I do not believe that public school systems accurately assess these principles, but I do believe that privately funded institutions can address these principles. I attended Catholic and a Non-denominational Christian school that was formerly Southern Baptist for a portion of my life. I also attended a public high school, and the curriculum was better developed in the private institutions. My conclusions after attending both kinds of institutions are that the private schools were better managed, better maintained, and had a more well-rounded curriculum. Additionally, I met individuals, teachers, staff, and clergy, that have molded my Academic and personal career in both Baptist and Catholic school. I always hear people scold nuns for smacking the top of a child's hand with a ruler when they are talking excessively in class or being disruptive in some other form, and I simply cannot believe that people actually do not believe that some form of discipline is necessary in a school system. Don't hurt yourselves, welfare liberals, this is not torture or unnecessary discipline, this is simply a body of educators ensuring that their students respect and value the education they are receiving. I may have gotten my knuckles smacked with a ruler once, but it was no more than that. I don't even clearly remember it ever happening because it was not a portion of the education that I obtained at Catholic school that was memorable. There were many other aspects of Catholic school that I cherish and value as the best education I could have received. And if it did happen and I was mercilessly slapped on the hand with a ruler, I'm sure I deserved it because I was probably chatting with one of my friends when I should have been listening to the nun speaking to the class. And really, welfare liberals, stop whining about idiotic things such as being smacked with a ruler, if it really hurts you that much to be smacked on the hand with a ruler, then you have much larger concerns that you need to address.

I also do not trust the government to 'aid the needy' as much as they are aiding themselves in the process. Trusting the government to 'aid the needy' means that we pay them tax money and trust that they spend it for charitable reasons in order to quell the poverty in this country. However, this is where that little portion of neoclassical liberalism that welfare liberalism doesn't really have the authority or logic to fight comes in, why not allow individual citizens of the United States to contribute their own charitable contributions to organizations they deem to be of direct relevance and importance to eliminating poverty and poor economic conditions for individuals? Why can the individual not be responsible for choosing the charity that their money is given to? I can never understand why welfare liberals act as though Americans are so hard-hearted they would never give some of their own money for the well-being of other less-fortunate Americans. That's just ridiculous and not grounded in logic. Welfare liberals would just like the government to control where our charitable donations go, and I disagree because I would like to choose where my own charitable donations will be apportioned. I believe that welfare liberals want to control charitable donations because they know that most charitable donations are given to an individual's church – which for some reason is not conceived as productive compared to giving it to the federal government. I hope welfare liberals are starting to see the flaw in their logic, but somehow I doubt it. Welfare liberals need to understand that churches are a very efficient and productive method for contributing to charity because many churches have set up shelters to feed, clothe, and house the homeless. Churches have historically been the best charity the world has ever known, and that will not be disputed because it simply cannot be. Americans may not agree with every charitable contribution by the Catholic Church, but opponents will not deny that the Catholic Church expends considerable time, manpower, and funds in order to promote a better lifestyle for many people (United States Institute for Peace). And the Catholic Church is definitely more efficient than the useless United Nations. Welfare liberals, you can disagree with the church and not give your charitable contributions to it, that is just fine; however, you do not have the authority to dictate to those of us who would like to give our charitable contributions to the church that we must give it to the government instead. It is illogical, irrational, and is not consistent with the idea of freedom – which welfare liberalism still claims to cling to.

Welfare liberalism also would like to 'regulate working conditions to promote workers' health and well-being.' I just don't agree with this because I think the individual worker is more than capable of looking out for their own health and well being and can assess when their job is not promoting their individual well-being, and, in light of this, the person will seek another job that will be more suitable.

"Only through such public support would the poor and powerless members of society become truly free." (p.71) Why does this seem to make good sense to welfare liberals? Why do they act as though this statement is cemented in the actual meaning of the word freedom? Freedom is the ability of the individuals to make their own choices, is it not? 'The poor and powerless members of society' are still free whether welfare liberals would like to believe it or not. They are free to succeed if they are willing to. If they would rather smoke crack, not have a job, and live in a gutter, then guess what? It is not the job of the federal government to fix their circumstance. I am not degrading every impoverished person in this country, but welfare liberalism does when it attempts to apportion levels of income from other members of society to allocate hard-earned resources to those who are not working. If a member of society does not have a job, then he/she should not get a welfare check from the government for sitting around and being unproductive. That may be 'freedom' as you define the word, welfare liberals, but it is not the actual definition of the word. Also, you are, without question, inhibiting the freedom of those individuals who do work and pay taxes when you institute these policies. That is why it is so illogical and irrational to subscribe to this ideology, this government intervention in Americans' lives, and then purport to support the 'freedom of the individual.' You do not. You support the freedom of the individual to not work and be supported by the more productive members of society.

This textbook states the neoclassical liberal philosophy adheres to the belief that these welfare liberalist policies inhibit the freedom of other individuals by promoting taxation which, in essence, takes property from one individual and transfer it to another. This is just malarkey. "Green responded that everyone gained freedom when he or she served the common good." (p.71) This textbook then states that 'positive freedom' is obtained when our 'ideal or "higher" selves' cooperate with one another. I am so incensed by these authors and their habitual need in this section to put their ideology above the idea of neoclassical liberalism. I suppose I shouldn't be since I do that quite often in this book; however, I am not writing a textbook. And when you're right, you're right. And you're wrong, welfare liberals. Neoclassical liberals believed that welfare liberalism led to policies that inhibit the freedom of other individuals by forcing them through government intervention to transfer their private property to other individuals, through taxes. I hate how these socialists and now welfare liberals always talk about working for the 'common good.' What does that even technically mean? The 'common good' of whom exactly? Everyone? Well, that's silly since not everyone will have the same 'common good.' People are different. Marxism/Communism/socialism and now welfare liberalism does not differentiate one individual from another and believes that people should be classified by the whole and not by the individual. We should be working for the 'whole,' even though we can never fully identify the whole or understand it, we should be working toward it. STOP IT, with that thought. An individual should be encouraged to work for their own profit and their own good. This is when people are the most productive in the economy -- when their incentive to achieve is their own well-being and the well-being of those other individuals in the world that they actually care about. The human mind does not have the capacity to truly care for every other person in the world – simply because it can never understand or know every person in the world. But individual people have individual dedications to people for personal reasons and those are the most strengthening and binding connections. Understanding this fact of life, it only makes sense to allow people to work for those immediate people in their life that they care about, whom they can see and touch and know personally. Additionally, the profit of an individual is used for an array of different things we must remember. For themselves, yes, but also their family, charities, loans, investments, and charges or bills – some unnecessary, but who are you to judge how an individual spends their own money?

The authors of this text then proceed to define human beings as beings with 'higher ideals' than pleasure-seeking and pain-avoidance. These ideas, they state, shape us as individuals and define how we believe we should be instead of how we actually are. "The laws and programs that help the unfortunate, smooth social relations, and restrict all-out competition are positive aids to liberty. They may restrict our selfish or 'lower' selves, but laws and programs of this sort encourage our 'higher' selves to realize our nobler and more generous ideals through social cooperation." (p.71) Social cooperation is not quite as wondrous and alluring as the welfare liberals make it sound. Also, I don't need social cooperation to show my 'higher' self – my more noble and generous ideals are shown when the federal government is not trying to control me. I can tell that the welfare liberals understand the flaw in their argument here, that's why they point it out and then claim to dismantle the logic by throwing out the 'lower' and 'higher' selves bit. The restraints, according to Ball/Dagger, limit only the freedom of our 'lower' selves. I'm entertained by this now because it simply is irrational, and I hope that it's as obvious to everyone else by this point in my explanation of liberalism why it is irrational. 'Our selfish or "lower" selves' may agree with this theory, but is not the definition of freedom that the individual has the right to make his/her own choices with his/her own life? I keep talking about the definition of the word because these welfare liberals keep skewing the definition of the word to mean what they want it to mean, but, unfortunately, the definition simply does not jive with the logic they employ. Welfare liberalism purports to be a more 'noble' of ideologies because it is looking out for the intentions of the less fortunate members of society – or so it CLAIMS. However, it is revoking the freedom of other individuals in the process and is not consistent with well-rounded logic.

My last section on this ideology will be to note a historical progression of political parties in this country. The Democratic Party, in the context of American history, has been the culprit of corruption. The Republican Party, while imperfect, has largely cleaned up the mess left by Democrats in their wake. Abraham Lincoln, the 16th President of the United States, who fought for the end of slavery and issued the Emancipation Proclamation, was a Republican. His opposition were democrats. Franklin D. Roosevelt, the 32nd President of the United States during the era of March 4, 1933- April 12, 1945 – during the Great Depression. FDR was a Democrat who implemented the "New Deal" otherwise known as the former welfare state in America. He created a mindset of dependence on the government and facilitated an economic society that gives handouts in place of rewarding good behavior. The 36th President, Lyndon B. Johnson who served in office from November 22, 1963, was even less equipped to handle the American economy and added to the economic downturn brought about by FDR and the democratic presidents that followed him. He implemented the Civil Rights Act, the Voting Rights Act, and medicare. And then there was the 39th President of the United States, Jimmy Carter, who was the first president since 1932 to lose re-election. Who came in to pick up after Jimmy Carter's mismanagement of the government? Ronald Reagan with George H.W. Bush as his Vice President – both Republicans, Bill Clinton, who has contributed to the economic collapse of the housing market with his involvement in the stabilization of Fannie Mae and Freddie Mac, bombed Iraq and whose responsibility before he high-tailed it out of office, and whose responsibility was it to take care of the situation in Iraq after President Clinton left office? President George W. Bush – another Republican.

In the past century, Democratic Presidents have contributed to society in a way that reflects a growing ideological trend of welfare-liberalism leaning towards socialism in the Party. Democratic politicians have been extremely disappointing as of recently – reference the Chapter on the Democratic Congress for more information. In this day and age, the Democratic Party is not the party of the upper-echelon of individuals. They are the power-hungry slumlords that have consistently and without regard fought to take rights away from certain American individuals in order to promote other individuals or a specific form of government control. That is not the government's job in the United States of America. It does not make sense to assume that it is the government's job to push equality, via control, through this country.

WAKE UP, people. If equality is truly what you desire, then you must appeal to the American public, sans corruption, and make it clear that you do not want equality for political reasons because that is not equality. Equality, as defined by the government, is not equality as defined by the American people. Equality does not mean that people of a certain race, color, ethnicity, nationality get things easier than those of other races, colors, ethnicities, and nationalities. Why does that even seem like a logical method to obtain equality? That does not promote equality. That promotes hatred and unrest within the American public. The only way for people in this country to be equal is for every person to be judged on their individual criteria and not on their race. People are free to succeed in this country, every person is. If you believe that you are oppressed by the American public and the American government, then you do not understand the true definition of the word oppression. Stop feeling sorry for yourself and study the life, ideals, and policies of Saddam Hussein – that man was an oppressor. You are not oppressed. You have free human rights (as of right now, granted in the Constitution of the United States), but you get no more than that because the government gives no one else more than that! You are not better than people of other races. You do not get special treatment unless we are allotted the same special treatment. People that fight for the 'uplifting' of a certain race are the reason for inequality in this country. People work for a living in this country, and if you do not work, then you do not earn a living. Every race should be given similar opportunities to succeed in this country; that is not up for debate. However, people get carried away with promoting a certain race and neglect to realize that they are just further dividing this country in their attempts.

CONSERVATISM

Conservatism as an ideology generally resists change within society because adherents would like to propose traditional solutions to problems that arise within the country. Conservatism can be used in array of different ways, to preserve a number of different notions or sets of ideals. Variations between conservatism usually form out of a desire to conserve some former mode of thought. When revolutionary thought, such as Marxism, is introduced, conservatives stand against these movements. These movements, conservatives believe, are not well planned or thought-out and can only be detrimental to the society. (p.87) Conservatives in America have been instrumental to the continued preservation of the Constitution of the United States of America. Modern day conservative minds, such as Ronald Reagan and Barry Goldwater, upheld the notions of neoclassical liberalism, a representative government, and the Constitution. Many constitutionalists are considered conservatives because they are attempting to conserve the tenants of the Constitution. I was blessed enough to be able to hear Justice Sandra Day O'Conner speak when I attended Wake Forest University. Supreme Court Justices are exceptional individuals who have not only gained intelligence and knowledge of the history of the Constitution and its logical and philosophical tenants, but they have also been instrumental in upholding these principles and overseeing the actions of the judicial branch. Justice O'Conner was extremely compelling, as the first female Supreme Court Justice elected by President Ronald Reagan. Another outstanding Supreme Court Justice to date is Justice Clarence Thomas, whom Barack Obama has personally taken to insulting and demeaning when asked the question of whom he would not have elected to the

Supreme Court. Justice Thomas is an exceptional individual who rose from poverty to become a renowned historical and political figure. Mark Levin invited Justice Clarence Thomas to be on his show, and I had the privilege of listening to his thoughts and opinions. He has a book out currently called "My Grandfather's Son" which describes the obstacles he overcame in order to become the man that he is today. This is a man that should be truly honored for his contribution to this country in upholding the laws of the land. Another book has been written detailing the magnificent scholarly works that Clarence Thomas has put forth in the Supreme Court; the book is called "Supreme Court Decisions by Clarence Thomas: 1991-2006" written by Henry Mark Holzer. If anyone has a question of the character of Justice Thomas, they are free to purchase these two books, which will inform them of the truths about the renowned individual they are demeaning. Barack Obama has absolutely no authority to criticize a man such as Clarence Thomas, an African-American man who has lived the American dream. Barack Obama is uninformed and uneducated on the decisions of the Supreme Court; the only thing he understands about Supreme Court Justice Thomas is that he wishes to uphold the laws outlined in the Constitution, and Barack Obama does not. Obama believes that the Constitution is a 'living' document that can be amended as he sees fit. It will not be amended according to Barack Obama's agenda; he will not get his filthy hands on our Constitution to taint and mangle it. He knows that if he were to try to un-lawfully amend the Constitution that Justice Thomas would stand in his way. Barack Obama made deplorable accusations about Supreme Court Justice Thomas's intelligence. In my humble opinion, he should apologize to Justice Thomas personally for his uninformed, unintelligent comment about Justice Thomas's involvement and achievements in the Supreme Court.

Constitutionalists are not the only form of conservatives in the United States of America currently. Quite the contrary, there are many variations of conservatism in America because people promote different beliefs and ethical obligations as those necessary to uphold. One important branch of conservatism is the socially conservative movement, also known as the Religious Right. These conservatives believe in upholding religious, generally Christian values and morals within society. They do not generally believe that government programs should be instituted in order to promote Christian values, but they do agree that government should not restrict government in any realm, even governmentally-funded programs. They believe in ideas such as the Ten Commandments in the Court Houses and Public School Systems. They stand against the progressive left's perpetual attempt to ban religion from school systems, and they are a central force of the pro-life movement. Ideologically, social conservatives would like to preserve moral values in society and encourage personal and moral responsibility of the individual. Individualist conservatives are closely related to the ideological platform of neoclassical liberalism and value very little involvement in the social and economic sectors of society.

The Ball/Dagger textbook's first example of conservatism is linking it to the hard-line communist movement of the Soviet Union. However, conservatism is not an ideology of corruption as that example would lead you to believe. Neoclassical liberals are now considered individualist conservatives for trying to preserve the views of that ideology. Conservatives believe it is important to be sure that change is necessary before the government jumps to the gun and fixes something that's not broken. As this text points out, there are many forms of conservatism and even two scholarly opponents pitted against each other could both be considered conservatives of some sort since they are both attempting to preserve a set of ideals. Ideologies are not painted in black and white. There are many variations, forms, and subtle distinctions between them. But these subtle distinctions can differentiate a social conservative who advocates government control over social aspects of life and an individualist conservative who advocates very little if any government intervention in the marketplace and the social sector. It can also differentiate a welfare liberal whose intentions begin as just a benevolent attempt to feed the hungry to a Marxist who believes that full-fledged Communism is the only route to achieve ultimate equality. These subtle distinctions must be noted and taken account for because they are very important in understanding a person's belief system and how those beliefs will affect their future actions.

Ball/Dagger explain the conservative criticism of the idea of welfare liberalism and socialism, but I would like to point out that it is not an 'abiding fear of mass society' that explains the conservative viewpoint on this; it is the desire of some individuals to be free of mass society and have their lives still function as normal. This is an important conservative notion to note though so I will more precisely explain it than this textbook did. In the welfare liberalist effort to aid the less fortunate, the end result usually produces stagnation because the people in the bottom rung of society are helped very little, not substantially by these programs, the top is mercilessly and perilously robbed of their income for these so-called 'noble' intentions, which results in a main populace that is worse off all-around in the long run.

Before the end of this section, I also must define Neo-conservatism. I always laugh a little bit every time I hear a welfare liberal attempt to throw out the brutal term "Neo-Con" as if it's some big ta-da insult to the Conservative movement, but when you understand the true definition of Neo-conservatism then it becomes quite comical that the liberals use this particular branch of conservatism to mock. Neo-conservatism is an ideology that has its roots in welfare liberalism; however, the individual has become disenchanted with the notions and beliefs of welfare liberalism so they switch to a more conservative ideology that still retains some of the same ideals, but not that many.

Ball/Dagger point out that neoconservatives are suspicious of Capitalism, but still admire its tenants and the economic form of government. They acknowledge the productive nature of a Capitalist society, but they are weary of leaving the market completely unregulated for fear of monopolies, oligopolies, and other forms of market control. They like Capitalism, but they are also critical of the unregulated productivity of a Capitalist economy.

The authors of the Ball/Dagger textbook are somewhere between welfare liberalism and socialism, but they're teetering way too close to Marxism to allow me to take them seriously. I'm also abashed at the way these authors degrade Capitalism. Their agenda is so firmly lodged into this book that it's almost nauseating. These authors do not even feel the need to capitalize the word 'Capitalism,' but they haven't missed an opportunity to capitalize the word 'Marxism.' However, the text notes that there are extreme consequences to Capitalism, but these 'potentially disastrous social and political consequences' of Capitalism are kept in check even by a limited federal government. That is the function of the government to ensure that Capitalism does not have 'disastrous social and political consequences.' I am also just sick to death of these moronic welfare liberals writing textbooks and then demeaning any progress made by Capitalism. Do you pseudo-intellectuals really not understand why you made a profit off of the textbooks you put your time and labor into writing? CAPITALISM. Capitalize the word because it's what paid for the computer you type out your fanatical praises of socialism/Communism/and Marxism on! Ungrateful brats.

Conservatism is largely an ideology of conservation of an age-old set of ideals and philosophies. There are harsh critics of every conservative movement, but then again, there are harsh critics of any ideological movement. Conservatism has been instrumental in the continued preservation of the Untied States of America because without these great political conservative thinkers, the Constitution may have been lost in the desire of deplorable politicians who would like to amend the Constitution just to get their name into the history of the document. Here is my advice to the liberal progressive movement and the Democratic Congress and politicians, keep your hands off of the Constitution until you can debate Justice Clarence Thomas on the historical premise of the cruel and unusual punishment amendment. Until then, you do not have the wit, intelligence, or authority to criticize a man such as Clarence Thomas. "What's interesting, and perhaps surprising, is that, 16 terms [after Justice Thomas had been inducted into the Supreme Court under harsh criticism of the extreme leftist movement], Thomas has quietly proved himself to be a serious constitutional thinker, who displays – for those sympathetic with his conservative jurisprudence, anyway – both great independence and considerable wisdom. Thomas forcefully rejects the notion, long favored by liberals, that the Constitution is a 'living document' and that Supreme Court justices should creatively adjust the meaning of its terms to afford more protection to minorities, to invent such unenumerated rights as the 'right to privacy,' and in general to promote 'progressive' ends that the Left can't seem to win at the ballot box. Instead, he has become the Court's most persuasive exponent of 'originalism' – the view that justices should interpret the Constitution as meaning with it did to those who read the document when it was framed. Since originalism is the jurisprudence most compatible with our republican form of government and the intentions of the Founding Fathers, it's looking as though the first President Bush got it right after all when he declared, upon nominating Thomas, that he was 'the best man for the job.'" (Presser)

CONCLUSIONS ON IDEOLOGIES

This is the end of the Chapter on ideologies, but this is not the end of considerable discourse and debate on the subject of ideologies and their relevance to modern day society. There are a lot of portions of these ideologies that I have not detailed, but I've given a good synopsis of most of them I think. I do debate the principles in a few of them, but I clearly distinguish the principles that I am fighting. Ideologies are always up for scrutiny and could really be considered ever-changing since the meaning must shift to fit the current economic climate of all of the countries on the globe. These are just general overviews of some of the ideologies that I deem to be relevant to the political election on November 4, 2008, but these are by no means all of them. Considerable credit should also be given to the liberation movements in this country. I did not detail liberation theology in detail, but these are the ideologies that have revolutionized the liberation of the individual by oppression from many different sectors. Many ideologies have been formatted to address the concept of freedom and how man can utilize this concept. Freedom is the most important concept when talking about ideologies because ideologies distribute a set of ideas that will essentially shape the way the government allocates the freedom to its citizens. In the United States of America, freedom is granted to every citizen in the Constitution of the United States. Many other countries are not so lucky. I will now move to talk about the Constitution of the United States of America in detail since it is the essential piece of the American pie and the key to our freedoms.

Chapter Four

The Constitution

The United States Constitution is a glorious and brilliant document outlining the functions of our government – down to every body of governments' specific granted powers. It also makes crystal clear the limitations of government and the democratic affiliation of the United States government to allow its citizens to participate in voting for politicians and specific issues of great interest to the American public. The wording of this document ensures that the people are in control of the government to the extent that the government's actions should always be representative of the people and reflect the majority's viewpoint. The intention is not to suppress the minority, but to encourage the minority to get involved and convince more people of their viewpoint. The majority rules in a democratic nation, and if this country still intends to tout its democratic principles, then it must retain some.

How can Americans retain democracy? Because whether democracy is necessarily good or bad is destined for scrutiny, but it is the way of life in the United States of America. I can only wearily write about democracy because I see the inherent flaws in the doctrine. The people, at times, will allow themselves to become uninformed and drone-like, and during these times, they may not use their best discretion when making decisions for this country – when voting for President of the United States, for example. I am not a person that will scream "GO VOTE" from the rooftops; I would rather an individual be able to recite some portion of the Constitution before they would be permitted to cast a vote. Then at least there is some consolation that the voter understands, even superficially, the laws guiding this land. The Constitution is a document that has laid out our laws; substantiated our inherent freedoms; and given us hope for a brighter future devoid of dictatorships and communism. Without the strength of this binding document, what does America have left that is uniquely hers?

The Constitution also permits the states' discretion on many issues. The Constitution values the opinion of the individual state – because the individual state understands the constituents of their population better than the whole. Another brilliant portion of the Constitution is the separation of federal and state powers. Article IV Section 4 of the Constitution is as follows: "The United States shall guarantee to every State in this Union a Republican Form of Government, and shall protect each of them against Invasion; and on Application of the Legislature, or of the Executive (when the Legislature cannot be convened) against domestic Violence." Americans must remember that the federal government exists to PROTECT the states. That is one of its main functions.

The Constitution allows for an amendment process. A two-thirds majority vote by both Houses of Congress can institute a Constitutional Amendment; however, this is never a decision that should be entered into whimsically. This is the United States Constitution that we're talking about. Most laws in this land can be passed without having to be amended into the Constitution. This is not a living document. This is the document our founding fathers put their intelligent minds and their revolutionary thinking into in order to concoct a very well-organized, substantial document that describes in detail the function of every legislative body in this country. This is why it is sickening the way these democrats want to revoke our 2nd Amendment right to gun ownership. This is the United States Constitution, Democrats. You had better be right if you alter something in the Constitution, that is the only thing that can be said to these people steadfastly attempting to revoke the right to gun ownership. If you amend the Constitution and gun violence rises, you will have amended the most sacred document in American History founded on the basis of protecting the individual when, in actuality, you have weakened the United States of America in your vain attempt to show authoritarian ideals.

My favorite part of the Constitution is the bill of rights. Now we are no longer talking about the federal and state governments' powers. We're talking about the rights of every American to life, liberty and freedom. Amendment 1 – Freedom of Religion, Speech, Assembly – "Congress shall make no law respecting an establishment of religion, or prohibiting the free exercise thereof; or abridging the freedom of speech, or of the press; or the right of the people peaceably to assemble, and to petition the Government for a redress of grievances." Beautiful. Simply beautiful. Separation of church and state, freedom of speech, and freedom to protest the government (peacefully) is all consolidated into one meaningful amendment. Americans shall stand against anyone that threatens to take these liberties because they are the breath of this country. This freedom that we as Americans so uniquely hold shall never be taken from us, except in death. Americans must understand how very important these freedoms are; how instrumental they have been to the life inside this country. Generations of Americans have subscribed to and lived by these very principles, and they have escaped persecution on the basis of religion, personal opinion, or disagreement with their government officials. This is America. Injustices may have occurred inside our walls, but we are ashamed of those injustices. We strive to minimalize those injustices until they are almost inconceivable. However, some people want to dwell on the past – the negativity of events that occurred decades or centuries ago. If equality is ever expected to survive in the United States, then we must put aside the differences of old that have divided Americans. Those differences are not important to the lives we live in 2008; there is no reason to perpetuate the belief that those injustices went unnoticed and were never rectified. Americans of every religion, creed, or doctrine; of every race, nationality, or ethnicity must unite inside the walls of this country if we ever hope to achieve success for the American dream and the American way of living.

Instead of uniting with the rest of the world, unite with your fellow Americans. Unite against injustice, if that is what you despise. Unite for truth, if that is what you seek. Unite for prosperity, if you believe this country holds more opportunity than any other nation. Americans are strong when united but weak when divided. Our enemies will lure Americans into believing they have noble intentions for our citizens, but they do not and they never have. America is a bastion of theories and principles designating the individual person as more important than the whole. Other legislative bodies in nations across the globe designate the government as the ultimate authority on something as fundamental as the individual choices people make in their day-to-day lives. These other forms of government, specifically socialism, Marxism, or Communism, suppress the voice and opinion of the individual and enhance the voice of the government over the individual.

So now that the George W. Bush presidency is coming to a close, I'm becoming more and more weary of the Patriot Act. I knew definitively the enemy that President Bush was fighting against and what the generous amount of surveillance technology granted in the Patriot Act would be for. I'm not so sure with Barack Obama. But our entire government needs to make sure not to violate the Constitution with the Patriot Act. Amendment 4 to the Constitution is 'Search and Seizure:' "The right of the people to be secure in their persons, houses, papers, and effects, against unreasonable searches and seizures, shall not be violated, and no Warrants shall issue, but upon probable cause, supported by Oath or affirmation, and particularly describing the place to be searched, and the persons or things to be seized." Americans need to pay attention to what these democrats are saying about the Patriot Act.

Amendment 9 to the Constitution states: "The enumeration in the Constitution, of certain rights, shall not be construed to deny or disparage others retained by the people." Democrats, remember this amendment to the Constitution when you put forth your resolutions to revoke our Constitutional rights. We will not let them go quietly, I assure you.

Amendment 10 – the final portion of the Bill of Rights – outlines the powers of the states and people. "The powers not delegated to the United States by the Constitution, nor prohibited by it to the States, are reserved to the States respectively, or to the people." Yet another brilliant segment of the Constitution. If the federal government is not delegated the power directly in the Constitution, any issue of relevance to the state or people is deemed the concern of the states and the people. So Americans, make sure to keep your congressman in line with your views. Write to them. Petition them. Watch them. They are speaking for your voice because we cannot hold a public election on every bill passed through the Congress. However, that does not mean the public should not be involved. Quite the contrary, in fact, the people in this country should involve themselves as much as they can in their local and state governments. These government officials get paid to represent YOU and your opinions. Remember that. As of July 31, 2007, your opinions and beliefs are still what propel our government to make the decisions they make.

OTHER IMPORTANT AMENDMENTS TO THE CONSTITUTION:

Amendment 13 – The Abolition of Slavery, "Section 1. Neither slavery nor involuntary servitude, except as a punishment for crime whereof the party shall have been duly convicted, shall exist within the United States, or any place subject to their jurisdiction. Section 2. Congress shall have power to enforce this article by appropriate legislation."

This Amendment is an excellent example of Americans recognizing injustice and wrong-doings going on within the country, and rectifying those by prohibiting those practices and delegating Congress to ensure that those practices be justly punished and, in essence, eliminated. African Americans and White Americans alike can recognize this as a cornerstone piece of legislation in the fight for freedom and justice within the walls of the United States of America. This legislation was passed in the year 1865.

Amendment 14 – Privileges and Immunities, Due Process, Equal Protection, Apportionment of Representatives, Civil War Disqualification and Debt: "Section One: All persons born or naturalized in the United States, and subject to the jurisdiction thereof, are citizens of the United States and of the state wherein they reside. No state shall make or enforce any law which shall abridge the privileges or immunities of citizens of the United States; nor shall any state deprive any person of life, liberty, or property, without due process of law; nor deny to any person within its jurisdiction the equal protection of the laws."

I just want to point out the due process of law noted in this amendment and admonish anyone from not adhering to this amendment. Without the due process of law, it is not the right of any United States citizen, government official or not, to "deprive any person of life, liberty, or property…nor deny to any person in its jurisdiction the equal protection of the laws."

Amendment 15 – "Rights Not to be Denied on Account of Race: Section 1. The right of citizens of the United States to vote shall not be denied or abridged by the United States or by any state on account of race, color, or previous condition of servitude. Section 2. The Congress shall have power to enforce this article by appropriate legislation."

Another important piece of legislation to the Civil Rights Movement.

Amendment 18 – Prohibition "Section 1. After one year from the ratification of this article the manufacture, sale, or transportation of intoxicating liquors within, the importation thereof into, or the exportation thereof from the United State and all territory subject to the jurisdiction thereof for beverage purposes is hereby prohibited. Section 2. The Congress and several states shall have concurrent power to enforce this article by appropriate legislation. Section 3. This article shall be inoperative unless it shall have been ratified as an amendment to the Constitution by the legislatures of the several states, as provided in the Constitution, within seven years from the date of the submission hereof to the states by the Congress."

See democrats, a good example for you to note: a group of legislators foolishly attempted to amend the Constitution. But this is not an Amendment to be proud of, nor did it help the American public in any way really since it was not instituted for long before it had to be revoked on the basis that it simply did not work. I am for the first and only time in this book going to quote Wikipedia – mostly because I think that on the topic of the U.S. Constitution that there are enough Constitutionalists in America checking to make sure that the definitions and explanations of the Constitution are not ridiculously mangled, and I like what they have to say on this subject of the 18th Amendment. "When Congress submitted this amendment to the states for ratification, it was the first time that a proposed amendment had a provision that placed a deadline on ratification. Because of many Americans' dismay at the emergence of Prohibition, there was a considerable growth in organized crime in the United States in response to public demand for illegal alcohol. Considered a very unpopular law, the amendment was subsequently repealed by the Twenty-First Amendment on December 5, 1933. It remains the only constitutional amendment to be repealed in its entirety." Now, if you attempt to amend the Constitution in order to repeal our second – or first, for that matter -- Amendment rights, I can assure you that it will not go well. 'A considerable growth in organized crime' occurred because the government attempted to ban alcohol. Democrats, think, please, for your sake, our sake, everyone's sake, just think about what you are proposing when you suggest to revoke the right to gun ownership. It will not work the flowery way you intend it to go. People tend to forget that the American public is vigilant and mindful of the things that go on in this country. I like to think of the American public as a sleeping tiger – we may not be at the pinnacle of our defense all the time, but threaten us, and we will tear you apart.

Amendment 19 – "Women's Right to Vote: The right of the citizens of the United States to vote shall not be denied or abridged by the Untied States or by any state on account of sex. Congress shall have power to enforce this article by appropriate legislation."

Oh I may have to jump for joy when I start talking about this Amendment. I love this Amendment for a lot of reasons, mostly because, well, I'm a woman, and I obviously believe that women have the right as an individual to cast a vote in any election. It's a foreign concept to me that women really did not have the right to vote less than a century ago. We've come a long way though, and we are pioneering right along. Women have learned in the past few decades that we can do anything and everything we set our minds to do as long as we apply ourselves and become competent, successful individuals on our own first. Women, collectively, have done a lot to show that our minds and spirits should be valued just as much as our ability to cook – (well, not really mine, but…) This Amendment propelled more women to exhibit in the workplace that we are just as equally competent to perform tasks as the opposite sex – whom we still tolerate and love dearly – most of the time. Females have been assimilated and integrated into the workplace as competent, successful individuals who, at the end of the day, can take care of themselves and their family. Thank God for the freedom of the United States of America that allows all of us to realize these amazing characteristics about ourselves. We are not oppressed. Our voices are heard if we wish to speak.

CONCLUSIONS:

I love the United States Constitution. Every American should because it is the only thing that has kept this country from falling into despair, disarray, and chaos. These powers delegated to the federal and state governments to protect and promote the individuals in society are good because there are proper checks and balances noted within the document that will ensure that this government never be overrun by corruption. This was a revolutionary document at the time of its founding and never has a single document been so instrumental in the development and continued prosperity of a nation. Americans, please continue to respect your Constitution and the ideals outlined within it because if you do not, then we are destined for a less productive future. We all must be able to recognize the importance of this sacred document and be able to reference it when individuals or movements threaten to take away the rights that we have been granted in the Constitution. This document will save us again as it has done countless times in the past. Do not mock the American commitment to these ideals because it is much more real than anyone subscribing to any other form of government could understand. This document is our freedom.

Chapter Five

The 2nd Amendment

The 2nd Amendment to the Constitution of the United States is as follows: "A well regulated Militia, being necessary to the security of a free State, the right of the people to keep and bear Arms shall not be infringed."

The right of Americans to bear Arms SHALL NOT be infringed. Read the wording of this amendment. The founding fathers made their intentions with this amendment abundantly clear. An American citizen has the right to own a firearm to defend oneself against foreign invaders OR the government itself. And to this very day, it is still necessary for a FREE State to have the right to bear arms. We must not allow the government to control the only firearms in this nation – well that does not include the control that criminals will have over law-abiding citizens since they will not forfeit the right to carry a gun even if it is the law of this land. Only abiding citizens will be forced to forfeit their firearms.

There is no logic to the democrat's position on firearms. None that I can find. So we will put regulations on guns to the point where law-abiding citizens will be unable to purchase a weapon for their own security, but our black market will grow exponentially. Let's recall a prime example of this sort of policy failing miserably: Prohibition of alcohol. You cannot ban a substance that is integrated so firmly into American tradition – be it alcohol or (over my dead body) guns. This is a fight for our core freedom as an American. We were given these rights at birth. Our Constitution instilled these rights into our mind, our very being. We WILL NOT allow our guns to be mercilessly ripped from our fingers by prying bureaucrats and politicians! We will stand and fight for these freedoms that are so brilliantly and precisely laid out by the founding fathers in the Great Constitution.

Let me make this clear to Barack Obama and the democratic Senators and Representatives that believe they hold the control over this country to institute the kind of amendment to the Constitution that will strip Americans of these very rights: you will never take the guns out of the South. We will stand against your ways, your callous absence of reason, and we will fight with our guns because YOU are the foreign invaders and government officials the founding fathers warned us would try to take our freedoms away. You use the façade of care, pretentious care for everyday Americans whom you want to save from themselves. You do not need to save us from anyone but yourself, Barack Obama, and of course the like-minded politicians who are bumbling through our Houses of Congress and our branches of government just itching to revoke this Constitutional freedom. But even more revolting is that these democrats simply do not care about Americans or our feelings toward the staunch injustice of bitter policies meant to stifle the American public. You want to stifle our freedoms, and you think we are ignorant enough to allow it without a second glance. We are not ignorant. WE ARE AMERICANS. And we know what it is to fight for our freedoms, we understand that so well that it is another one of our American ideals bred into our very being. We will fight you and your socialist policies and your anti-gun toting garbage.

I had never seriously considered purchasing a firearm until a news story was relayed to me via conservative talk radio. A vote went through the Supreme Court intending to ban guns to an extent in Washington D.C. Barack Obama supported this amendment until the verdict came in. It was a 5-4 verdict in opposition of allowing the bill to go through Congress. FIVE to FOUR. That is how close Washington D.C. Americans came to potentially losing this freedom that is taken for granted everyday. I am a law-abiding citizen with every right to own a firearm, and I assure you if it is ever imminent that the right will be stripped of me, I will stand in line all night, camp out in front of my local gun store, and stock up in order to preserve the right that I, as an American, will always hold.

Americans will not be stripped of the right to gun ownership because it is intrinsically necessary to preserving the state of security in this country. Hence why it is outlined so concisely in the actual Amendment. Reread the Amendment to the Constitution. The right to bear arms goes much deeper than a comforting sense of individual security, Americans must also be able to fight back against their government – particularly in times of corruption. The founding fathers learned one important thing in their voyage to this country and its founding, checks and balances are critical to stability because without those, we are without real protection. The 2nd Amendment is a part of the checks and balances system in this country that many Americans may not even realize. Without the ability to form a Militia against a corrupt government, we lose the ability as Americans to disagree with corrupt politicians. It is an animalistic right, but it keeps the government in check to some extent. Without the right to bear arms, the right of the people to rebel against corruption is no longer an option.

CONCLUSIONS:

I do not believe that any other articles or text need to be cited in this Chapter on the 2nd Amendment. I believe that the Constitutional failure of the 18th Amendment is proof enough to justify my point that revoking the right to gun ownership simply will not work in this country. I also believe that this piece of legislation was laid out so precisely in the Constitution – I'm referencing the 2nd Amendment now – that it really only bears repeating and then the recognition of how poorly it will go not only for the American public but mostly, for the American government. If the United States Government does not recognize this warning and stop threatening to revoke the right to gun ownership, then we will revolt. That is all that you need to know. This Amendment and the Eighteenth are also discussed at length in the Chapter titled Constitution.

Chapter Six

The Democratic Congress

In order to properly analyze the effect of the Democratic Congress on our current economic and social predicament in this country, the Congressional voting records must be critically analyzed. This is not an easy task, but I've done research on bills containing issues that I believe are of particular relevance to understanding the impact of this Congress. I cannot list every resolution or bill that has gone through the House of Representatives in the 110th Congress, the breadth of that task is simply too massive. Not to mention that many of their bills are recognitions, appreciations, and commendations to specific American persons of great contribution to the well being of this country. However, I have made many interesting discoveries while researching these bills, and the most efficient way I can think to organize the Congressional bills of the Democratic Congress is to list the bill or resolution and the title, then underneath give a brief description of the tenants and merit of the document. If the Congressional year is not specified when the bill is listed, assume the vote to have occurred in the current 110th Congress. Let's begin with the first concurrent resolution, a resolution passed by both houses of the legislative body, the 110th Congress. (These bills and resolutions are listed in the Washington Post Archives, which also links to the Library of Congress for full-text excerpts of the bills.)

H. CON. RES. 1 – "Regarding consent to assemble outside the seat of government."

This bill authorizes the Houses of Congress to assemble 'outside the District of Columbia if, in their opinion, the public interest shall warrant it.' This resolution passed the House on January 4, 2007, the day after new members were inducted into Congress and the 110th Congress began. Why do the congressmen feel the need to assemble outside of Washington D.C.? Our government is centrally located in Washington D.C. and laws, bills or resolutions passed through Congress should be addressed in our nation's capital. This amendment also seems to provide for private meetings throughout the country.

CONGRESS ON THE WAR IN IRAQ

H CON RES 63 – Disapproving of the decision of the President announced on January 10, 2007, to deploy more than 20,000 additional United States troops to Iraq.

Congress opposed the surge from the start. Here is the proof. So therefore, it makes quite a bit of sense that they should get absolutely no credit for the masterful way the Surge has worked in Iraq. They should also get no credit for being consistent since the **107th Congress** passed **H J RES 114** authorizing the President's use of military force in Iraq -- both houses of Congress voted and approved this bill. It is entitled *"Authorization for Use of Military Force Against Iraq Resolution of 2002."* The Republican and Democrat majority opinion on this bill was "Yes." Democratic Senators such as Joseph Biden, Maria Cantwell, Tom Daschle, John Edwards, Dianne Feinstein, John Kerry, Joseph Lieberman, Zell Miller, Harry Reid, Jay Rockefeller, and, of course, Hillary Clinton voted "Yes" to this bill. Note that Barack Obama did not vote period on this bill. He was not in the Senate at the time. He likes to misrepresent that fact. Lincoln Chafee was the only Republican Senatorial member that voted in opposition to this bill. Congress has been extremely inconsistent when it comes to this war and it is for one bitingly obvious reason, it is all contingent on how public opinion reflects on the war at the time. I personally think it also has quite a bit to do with how much the American public allows themselves to be brainwashed by the mainstream media and misled to believe things about this war that are simply untrue or fail to detail an appropriate version of the story.

108ᵀᴴ CONGRESS, 1ˢᵀ SESSION, S. CON. RES. 31:

Whereas Saddam Hussein has failed to comply with United Nations Security Council Resolutions 678, 686, 687, 688, 707, 715, 949, 1051, 1060, 1115, 1134, 1137, 1154, 1194, 1205, 1284, and 1441:

Whereas the military action now underway against Iraq is lawful and fully authorized by the Congress in section 3(a) of Public Law 107-243, which passed the Senate on October 11, 2002, by a vote of 77-23, and which passed the House of Representatives on that same date by a vote of 296-133;

In this particular Senatorial Concurrent Resolution, Americans can view a brief outline of United Nations Security Council Resolutions that Iraq had mercilessly violated time after time. Diplomacy is always at work in the United Nations of course, and astonishingly enough, it failed. What really gets me fired up about the United Nations is that they relentlessly sanctioned, mandated, and resolved the Iraqi government – specifically Saddam Hussein, and when they noticed that none of their resolutions were being carried out, what did the UN accomplish? NOTHING. The UN is a peacekeeping body by nature. It was not intended to facilitate wars or condone military action, so what is the purpose of this largely useless legislative body that the United States not only funded the development of but also implemented and housed in our own country? Peace-KEEPING. Not peace-making. In times of peace, the UN can dilly-dally around and implement their useless resolutions all over other countries. However, there comes a point when peace does not occur simply because the UN slaps a couple resolutions and mandates on a corrupt government. Dictatorships do not know the American version of peace and freedom. They are foreign to our ideas and beliefs. I'm even more incensed by the UN's complete lack of effectiveness, and then the audacity of the body of legislators housed in our own country to then turn in opposition to our efforts in Iraq. They have got to be the most useless organization this country has ever housed. Well, aside from bureaucracies in general. And what in the blue blazes does Barack Obama think the UN has done in exhausting ALL diplomatic efforts with these psycho-paths and dictators running the corrupt Middle Eastern governments? Here's an important lesson for Barack Obama to learn in diplomacy: WE TRIED. IT FAILED. This is the United States of America. Diplomacy is an ally, but the United States Military is an irreplaceable resource to this country. Barack Obama seems to believe that these neighboring countries across the Atlantic foster so many good intentions for United States citizens; however, I don't really understand that logic since that mindset would be completely out of character for Europeans. The Europeans were never fond of us before, mainly for jealousy purposes, so why would we believe that they have suddenly become benevolent to American intentions? Our ancestors high-tailed it directly out of Western Europe to form a new, free government. Europeans haven't forgotten that fact, either, and they still act offended by it. But good, the Europeans should be offended, look at the success and happiness of the American people as compared to the French, English, German, or Russian people. Another reason the Europeans seem to be so fond of Barack Obama is because he's a Marxist, and even Europeans can put two and two together to figure out a Marxist will mean the complete collapse of the American economy. The Europeans will marvel at that. Not to mention that he looks and acts like a superficial celebrity, that is right up the European alley, so to speak. But that's quite enough about the Europeans.

Also, note this section of **108ᵗʰ Congress S CON RES 31**, "Whereas the military action now underway against Iraq is lawful and fully authorized by the Congress in section 3(a) of Public Law 107-243." Interesting. The Congressional authorization is even noted in later bills, yet they can never fully admit to their instrumental role in the ongoing military presence in Iraq and Afghanistan. They never take responsibility for their actions, these democrats. It is impossible to get one to admit to the truth behind their votes and the actual impact these votes have on Americans.

H. CON. RES 14 – "EXPRESSING THAT CONGRESS HAS THE SOLE AND EXCLUSIVE POWER TO DECLARE WAR."

Whereas the President should present to Congress the question of whether to declare war as provided for in section 8 of article I of the Constitution of the United States; and

Whereas when the valiant men and women of the United States military are away from home to fight a war, to protect the peace, or to enforce disarmament, they will have the full support of the Congress, and Congress will take every possible step to ensure that they are protected from potential attacks and a negative environment, they need to do their jobs effectively and efficiently , and they are brought home safely as soon as practicable.

Magnificent. So now the inconsistent Congress that on October 11, 2002 voted to authorize military action in Iraq, then later revoked that law, and opposed all progress in the war since then has now granted themselves 'the sole and exclusive power to declare war.' I'm so glad that a legislative body with so much foresight and intelligence now has the sole power to declare war. After they passed the concurrent resolution authorizing military action, weren't the democrats complaining about having a 'lack of intelligence?' That's just funny. Of course the democrats have a lack of intelligence. That's nothing we need them to alert us to. The Congress claimed to have been misled by President Bush and given inaccurate or incomplete documentation of the intelligence of foreign countries. However, this is a misrepresentation of the facts. I will now briefly list the intelligence gathered before September 11, 2001 on the looming terrorist attacks. Keep in mind I'm referencing the knowledge of the United States Foreign Intelligence Agency on the September 11 attacks, not potential future attacks on the United States by Iraq – that will be discussed later. Since there have been no attacks on any United States territory since September 11, 2001, I'm satisfied that the foreign intelligence agency has done their job. However, it is important to note that the facts state that they did their job even before the September 11th attacks. Also, keep in mind Barack Obama's vote in the Senate against funding the "Foreign Intelligence Surveillance Act of 2007." That vote is particularly troubling.

Here's a quotation from the 9/11 Commission Report:

"As 2001 began, counterterrorism officials were receiving frequent but fragmentary reports about threats. Indeed, there appeared to be possible threats almost everywhere the United States had interests – including at home. Information is collected through several methods, including signals intelligence and interviews of human sources, and gathered into intelligence reports. Depending on the source and nature of the reporting, these reports may be highly classified – and therefore tightly held – or less sensitive and widely disseminated to state and local law enforcement agencies." (P. 254)

Another excerpt from the 9/11 Commission Report:

"In the spring of 2001, the level of reporting on terrorist threats and planned attacks increased dramatically to its highest level since the millennium alert. At the end of March, the intelligence community disseminated a terrorist threat advisory, indicating a heightened threat of Sunni extremist terrorist attacks against U.S. facilities, personnel, and other interests."

H. CON. RES. 319 – "Recognizing March 19, 2008, as the fifth anniversary of the Iraq war and urging President George W. Bush to begin an immediate and safe redeployment of United States Armed Forces from Iraq."

This bill also states the following:

"Whereas President Bush and his Administration continue to carelessly spend billions of dollars a month in Iraq, diverting critically needed funding for health care, education, strengthening the Nation's bridges and infrastructure, and assisting Americans coping with an economic recession."

How has the democratic congress gained any authority to lecture President Bush on irresponsible spending? I suppose they will say it is the trillion-dollar deficit in this country, but they have done absolutely nothing to alleviate the debt or even mollify it. They have cut programs in order to pave the way for many other federally funded programs. They have put hundreds of earmarks in legislation for funding their programs. They have halted any effort to bring down fuel prices. They have turned their noses up at offshore drilling. They have increased taxes, and they have increased inflation. And yet they are still arrogant enough to dictate to President Bush how to fund a war they clearly do not understand. In this bill, the wording indicates programs that will alleviate economic concerns for everyday Americans; however, that pipe dream seems quite contrary to most of the legislation that they have passed thus far.

CONGRESS ON ENERGY EFFICIENCY –
INCLUDING CRUDE OIL

I will first cite an article (a World Tribune Special) entitled "GOP conservatives: Democrats' record is one of blocking U.S. energy supply." This document was prepared by the Republican Study Committee – 'a group of over 110 House Republicans organized for the purpose of advancing a conservative social and economic agenda in the House of Representatives.'

"In light of rising crude oil prices, the resulting spike in gas prices, and the continued reliance on energy supplies from unfriendly or unstable regions of the world, the RSC has prepared the following policy brief summarizing the Democrat pattern of blocking attempts to increase the supply of American energy and actively promoting policies that would make American energy less available, more expensive, and thus less affordable for poor and middle class Americans.

It's basic economics. When demand exceeds supply, the price goes up. One way to bring the price back down when worldwide demand is soaring-or to at least slow the rate of the increase-is to increase supply. Despite these widely understood realities, Democrats continue to speak ill about gas prices yet do ill about energy supplies. Even more disconcerting is the Democrat unwillingness to increase American energy supplies, as they block proposal after proposal aimed at allowing more energy supplies to be extracted from the American and Canadian ground, yet assert that OPEC should be sued for not increasing its exports. The logic simply does not work.

Like it or not, petroleum is the backbone of America's transportation energy today. If you need an ambulance to get you to the hospital, it won't be fueled by wind-powered batteries. If a school teacher needs to drive to work, her car's engine won't run on solar. And if a businessman needs to fly overseas on short notice, his plane won't get off the ground using biofuels. Alternative energy sources may be more prevalent and economical far in the future, but for now and perhaps decades to come, if America wants to increase or even just maintain its standard of living, if America wants to stay ahead of the rapidly developing economies in Asia and elsewhere, then America needs petroleum-and lots of it. "

"Most people understand that petroleum does not grow on trees. It's deep in the ground, and it doesn't come up by itself. It's in some parts of the world and not others. To get more petroleum over time, it's necessary to get it from more places.

The good news is that America is teaming with untapped petroleum resources-trillions and trillions of barrels. This point is not debatable. The bad news is that Democrats believe that whether such energy resources should be recovered is debatable. As demonstrated below, Democrats have not just been neutral on increasing American energy exploration, extraction, and refining-they have opposed it. Such Democrat energy intransigence comes at the expense of the poor and middle class. "

I will focus in this book only on drilling in ANWR; however, it is good to be aware that there have been subsequent other resolutions about oil drilling not directly related to ANWR that the Democrats have also prohibited from passing through Congress. ANWR is an acronym for 'Alaska's Arctic National Wildlife Refuge,' where "initial surveys show the presence of massive amounts of petroleum-upwards of a million barrels a day." To mirror this article, I will now list an assortment of House resolutions put forth by Republican members of Congress in order to facilitate the growth of this potential industry.

H R 39 – January 4, 2005, Rep. Don Young (R-AK) introduced a bill to repeal the prohibition against the production of oil and gas from ANWR and any leasing or development leading to such production.

H R 6 – April, 21, 2005, the House passed a bill to allow oil and gas leasing in ANWR. 90% of Republicans voted for the bill, while 80% of the Democrats voted against it. The provision was removed from the bill before it was signed into law.

H R 4004 – October 6, 2005, Representative Ron Paul (R-TX) introduced this bill to repeal the prohibition against the production, leasing and development of oil and gas from ANWR. This legislation has also been reintroduced as **H R 2415** in the 110th Congress.

H R 4562 -- May 23, 2006, Representative Marilyn Musgrave (R-CO) introduced a bill to direct the Bureau of Land Management to establish an oil and gas-leasing program in ANWR and conduct two lease sales there before October 1, 2010.

H R 5429 – May 25, 2006, the House passed a bill to repeal the proscription against the production or leasing of oil and gas resources from the ANWR and to provide extensive environmental safeguards for such production. 87% of Republicans voted for the bill, while 86% of the Democrats voted against it.

H R 5890 – July 26, 2006, Representative Devin Nunes (R-CA) introduced a bill to repeal the prohibition against production of oil and gas from ANWR and any leasing or development leading to such production.

H R 3089 – July 18, 2007, Representative Mac Thornberry (R-TX) introduced this legislation to repeal the prohibition against producing oil and gas from ANWR.

Republicans have also supported drilling on the OCS – the Outer Continental Shelf – 'the lands under the waters surrounding the United States, most of which are statutorily off limits to energy development.' I am not going to list all of those resolutions, but you can view all 13 bills introduced by House Republicans in the paper copy of this article.

Now, I will discuss the lengths that the Democrats in Congress have gone to stifle any energy exploration off of our coasts, as if their voting records on these energy bills alone is not proof enough.

"Democrats have consistently blocked all efforts to allow energy exploration and extraction in ANWR, despite the fact that such activity already occurs in wildlife refuges across the country without destroying the affiliated ecosystems. On February 2, 2005, Representative Ed Markey (D-MA) introduced a bill **(H R 567)** to designate oil-rich lands within ANWR as wilderness and components of the National Wilderness Preservation System, thus erecting another barrier to energy extraction there. Representative Markey has reintroduced the legislation in the **110ᵗʰ Congress (H R 39).**

On April 20, 2005, Representative Ed Markey (D-MA) offered an amendment **(H Amdt 72)** to **H R 6** to strike the provisions of the underlying bill allowing oil and gas exploration in ANWR. 85% of Democrats voted for the amendment, while 87% of the Republicans voted against it. Democrats have also put forth 9 pieces of legislation designed to block production of oil on the Outer Continental Shelf (OCS). Reference this article if you would like to know the exact bills that passed through Congress concerning this. "Democrats have consistently blocked expanding the development of 'unconventional' petroleum resources, despite their promise to deliver more fuels from American sources to meet today's energy demands, while decreasing the need to import oil from unstable and unfriendly nations."

H RES 1304 – "Providing for consideration of the bill (H.R. 6052) to promote increased public transportation use, to promote increased use of alternative fuels in providing public transportation and for other purposes."

The House did pass this bill, though. Surprisingly enough, the democrats' solution to the oil crisis is 'increased public transportation use' and 'increased use of alternative fuels in providing public transportation.' I want to slap these democrats. Bring them back to reality of life in America in 2008. This is why I continue stating that Barack Obama and like-minded democratic individuals are completely out of touch with southern and suburban lifestyles. Where I live, it is impossible to use public transportation unless you live in the downtown or campus area of the city and commute to another part of the same city. People drive cars here. I know very few people that have ever used public transportation in this area, much less on a regular basis. But there's a more important, glaring reality these democratic nitwits need to realize, we do not want to use public transportation nor will we welcome mass transportation. So you have stifled our cries for help with gas prices, only to also make it abundantly clear to every single person that you do not give one iota what gas prices are as long as it helps your environmental and socialist cause.

H.R. 1252 – "To protect consumers from price-gouging of gasoline and other fuels, and for other purposes."

Democratic Vote – 228 "Yes" 1 "No" Republican Vote – 56 "Yes" and 140 "No"

This must be a last-ditch attempt from some of the Democrats to increase their popularity ratings at home since they have failed to provide any necessary appropriations that would alleviate the concern of rising fuel prices in this country. The vote count was 228 Democrats voted "Yes," and 1 Democrat opposed. Republicans largely opposed this bill voting 140 "No" and 56 "Yes."

H CON RES 398 Passed/Agreed To in the House Status: "*On Adjourning the Houses of Congress on July 31, 2008.*"

On July 14, 2008, President George W. Bush "lifted an executive ban on offshore drilling that has stood since his father was President (CBS)." Ever since the lift of this presidential ban, the Democratic Congress has been pressured by all sectors of the Republican administration to have an up or down vote on offshore drilling. However, on July 31, 2008, before a vote could be had on offshore drilling, the Democratic Congress voted to adjourn until September. 213 Democrats voted to adjourn Congress without a vote, 17 Democrats voted "No," and 6 did not vote at all. The Republicans unanimously voted to stay for a vote on offshore drilling (0-195-4). The end tally for votes is as follows: 213 "Yes" votes, 212 "No" votes, with 10 not voting.

As Rep. Anthony Weiner – elected by 'Stretch' Pelosi to do her dirty work -- screamed "the Ayes have it," a roar came from the crowd – from the Republican Congressmen. "NO!" They shouted as Speaker Pelosi and the democratic leadership silenced their voices – not only through their actions by not allowing a vote on offshore drilling, but also by the egregious miscarriage of justice that followed afterward. Over 100 Republican Senators planned to stay until Midnight if they had to, detailing their plans for energy efficiency and offshore drilling in ANWR. But the lights were turned off on these valiant men. The microphones shut off, and the CSPAN cameras were taken away. Never before has something like this happened in the House of Congress. Over 50 Republican Congressmen stayed after the lights and cameras were shut off to continue with the legislation they know to be of vital importance to the American public. Tourists were giving standing ovations to the Congressmen that stayed, expressing their gratitude for these men and women that would not be silenced by the shift-less, spineless agenda of the Democratic Congress. I listened to a clip of this disgusting scene. I heard the roar of displeasure, anger, and sheer frustration as the Republicans fought in every way they knew how to open up debate and discourse on offshore drilling. In the anger I feel toward the Democrats for their egregious actions and blatant disrespect to every American citizen in this country, I also feel a sense of triumph. These Republicans stood up to this disgusting excuse for leadership in the Houses of Congress. I would like to commend every single congressman or woman that stood up to these actions – to say to these slumlords, that Americans will not take this disrespect lying down. I have been saying for weeks that there will be a revolution in this country if a Marxist takes over the White House, and after this display from the House of Representatives – specifically Speaker Pelosi – I am certain that it will come to that. So gear up, Democrats, because you will be fighting a much more intelligent and resourceful breed of human. You will not win. Please do not give yourselves too much credit; you should fear your enemy in this country. You have not converted everyone in this country to your line of thinking, and we have voices that can scream just as loud as your own, in my opinion, even louder as we are the voices of reason. And do not confuse yourselves, we will be screaming for freedom, liberty, and the pursuit of happiness. You will be screaming for superficiality, socialism, and political correctness, but you will never silence us. You will NEVER silence the American public.

I got most of this information from the Mark Levin Show (applaud, kudos, and all the necessary commendations to that show…I absolutely love it and can't wait to listen tomorrow), and he had Congressman Mike Pence of Indiana on the show after this event occurred. Rep. Pence played a critical role in the mini-revolution the Republicans presented to the House of Representatives when they adjourned Congress without an up or down vote on offshore drilling. Rep. Pence informed us that Speaker Pelosi allowed talk of a German resolution to cut off the debate on oil drilling. But he had this to say in response to these actions, "They are not going to silence the voice of the American people in the American people's House. One [Congressman] after another called on Speaker Pelosi to bring this Congress back and give us an up or down vote on American oil."

We will now wait to see if President George W. Bush exercises his power to reconvene Congress, even in light of the fact that they have given themselves a paid vacation.

An update to the above situation: Sean Hannity just played a clip of 'Stretch' Pelosi (Levin) giving a brief overview of how she never plans to allow a vote on this bill because it is contrary to the environmentalist principles that she believes the 110th Congress was instituted to address. She said she would not surrender the gavel to this legislation. She said she would like to 'reduce our dependence on foreign oil and save…er…reverse global warming.' She then said that she would not promote legislation contrary to those principles, and she does not understand 'why we're spending all this time on a parliamentary tactic when nothing is at stake but the planet – the air we breathe, and the air our children breathe.' This woman is a joke. A laughing stock. A complete and utter failure as the Speaker of the House of Representatives. And I am just as disappointed as you are because I am a woman and I would really like to have seen the first female Speaker of the House make substantial improvements to our government, but all this hag has done is promote her political and financial agenda while simultaneously ignoring her constituency and the rest of the American public. She is a witch and should be tried and burned as such.

H R 2643 – "Agreeing to Interior, Environment, and Related Agencies Appropriations"

The House has put forth 24 failed attempts on this bill. Note that none of the 'Interior, Environment, and Related Agencies' are related to alternative fuels. I didn't delve very far into this legislation but I do know that the President of the United States opposed this legislation for the following reasons (among others):

"The President also objected to this bill because it includes an irresponsible and excessive level of spending and includes other objectionable provisions. The President has called on Congress to reform the earmarking process that has led to wasteful and unnecessary spending. Specifically, he called on Congress to provide greater transparency and full disclosure of earmarks, to put them in the language of the bill itself, and to cut the cost and number by at least half. The administration opposes any efforts to shield earmarks from public scrutiny and urges Congress to bring full transparency to the earmarking process and to cut the cost and number of earmarks by at least half."

CONGRESS ON THE ECONOMY

In reference to the Democratic Congress's direct impact on the United States Economy, it would be impossible to pinpoint the full impact of one legislative body on the entire economy. The Congress and the President of the United States cannot directly affect the economy negatively unless policies are implemented that thwart economic prosperity and efficiency. An example of a policy that could propel the economy into recession – this policy would need to be accompanied by other policies intended to deplete Capitalism's ideals -- would be an egregious increase in the minimum wage – as this would cut a proportional number of jobs to the amount of increase. Minimum wage is theoretically unnecessary in a Capitalist economy. Wage compensation should equal the suitability of an individual for a particular position. Of course, many people disagree as to what that should be, but Capitalistic theories state that the market will be able to rectify any substantial injustice in wage compensation. The federal government does not need to be directly involved in this. And if they do involve themselves, then they should be considered responsible for the imminent blow to the unemployment rate. The responsibility should be given to the states to decide a fair minimum wage for their specific state because the standards of living in different areas of this country vary dramatically. That is what a federal minimum wage law can never take account for, and why it should be the sole and exclusive right of the state to analyze their business climate and determine what is a fair and decent wage for even the most menial of jobs.

H R 2 – "Fair Minimum Wage Act of 2007"

"This bill would increase the federal minimum wage from $5.15 an hour to $7.25 an hour over two years. It would increase the minimum wage in three increments. Sixty days after enactment, the minimum wage is to be raised to $5.85. A year after that it will be $6.55, and a year after that it will be $7.25. This would be the first change to the Fair Labor Standards Act of 1938 since 1997 when the federal minimum wage was increased from $4.75 to $5.15 an hour. The bill would also apply the federal minimum wage to the Northern Mariana Islands, a territory of the United States. The legislation passed in the Senate on February 1, 2007, on a 94-3 vote. The Senate measure includes about $8 billion over 10 years in tax breaks for businesses like restaurants, which is likely to be a sticking point when the chamber tries to reconcile its version with the House. The House passed its version of the bill on January 10, 2007, with a vote of 315-116. Every House Democrat voted in favor of the proposal along with 82 Republicans." (Washington Post)

H RES 1265 – Providing for Consideration of the Bill (H.R. 5749) to Provide for a Program of Emergency Unemployment Compensation. Passed in the House.

I understand that the Democratic Congress feels the need to pass a bill with emergency unemployment compensation, I just wonder if they understand why this is necessary. I already explained it above, but it is because of H R 2 the incremental increase in minimum wage. Here is what systematically happens every time a federal minimum wage is implemented in a Capitalist economy; an increase in the unemployment rate – usually the jobs easiest to cut out of the economy. American businesses must yield a profit in order to maintain a functioning marketplace. These businesses will not allow themselves to turn over no profit because that will be the collapse of the business – and the loss of every job the business has to offer. Since it makes logical sense that the business would not allow themselves to go out of business, how will they compensate for increased taxes, the revoking of subsidies, and an increase in how much they must compensate individuals for the jobs that they do? They will cut jobs. And the marketplace will be forced to cut a lot of them to stay afloat when policies that hinder their progress and development are implemented by the federal government.

H RES 3043 – "Departments of Labor, Health and Human Services, and Education, and Related Agencies Appropriations Act, 2008 (Enrolled as Agreed to or Passed by Both House and Senate.)"

There have been 67 votes thus far on the House Resolution 3043 'making appropriations for the Departments of Labor, Health and Human Services, and Education, and related agencies for the fiscal year ending September 30, 2008 and for other purposes. This is the document that has yielded the most votes by members of Congress so I will give a brief outline of the appropriations passed through the House and Senate for the 2008 budget (in this specific bill). I will try to be as comprehensive as I can when detailing how funding is dispersed through agencies, but, this task is almost more difficult than simply researching the voting records because so many appropriations for the budget are made in one singular bill.

Title I of this bill focuses on the Department of Labor – the Employment and Training Administration. The bill specifically addresses appropriations to be made for the 2008 fiscal year in reference to the "Workforce Investment Act of 1998 'WIA,'" and other appropriation bills such as "the Denali Commission Act of 1998, and the Women in Apprenticeship and Non-Traditional Occupations Act of 1992." **H RES 3043** act details that $3,618,940,000 dollars of the federal budget for 2008 be distributed 'for grants to States for adult employment and training activities, youth activities, and dislocated worker employment and training activities." This Title also allows for $483,371,000 'for federally administered programs.' There are also provisions in this title made for Community Service Employment for Older Americans and, of course, federal unemployment benefits and allowances. Title I "State Unemployment Insurance and Employment Service Operations" states the following: "For authorized administrative expenses, $90,517,000, together with not to exceed $3,337,506,000 which may be expended from the Employment Security Administration Account in the Unemployment Trust Fund ('the Trust Fund')." This title also appropriates $437,000,000 to the unemployment trust fund and other funds. In my opinion, the government should be funding incentive programs for new job training rather than raising the unemployment trust fund by $437 million dollars. It then goes on to list a variety of salaries and expenses that have been granted to the Department of Labor.

Title II of HR 3043 appropriates monies to the Department of Health and Human Services for Health Resources and the Services Administration. "$7,235,468,000, of which $317,684,000 shall be available for construction and renovation (including equipment) of health care and other facilities and other health-related activities as specified in the statement of the managers on the conference report accompanying this Act, and of which $38,538,000 from general revenues, notwithstanding section 1820 (j) of the Social Security Act, shall be available for carrying the Medicare rural hospital flexibility grants program." And so on and so forth. If you are curious about the exact wording if the entire legislation, research it. This title then goes on to appropriate funding to the National Cancer Institute, National

Heart, Lung, and Blood Institute, National institute of Dental and Craniofacial Research, National Institute of Diabetes and Digestive and Kidney Diseases, National Institute of Neurological Disorders and Stroke, National Institute of General Medical Sciences, National Institute of Child Health and Human Development, National Eye Institute, National Institute of Environmental Health Sciences, National Institute on Aging, National Institute of Arthritis and Musculoskeletal and Skin Diseases, National Institute on Deafness and other Communication Disorders, National Institute of Nursing Research, National Institute of Alcohol Abuse and Alcoholism, National Institute on Drug Abuse, National Institute of Mental Health, National Human Genome Research Institute, National Institute of Biomedical Imaging and Bioengineering, National Center for Research Resources, National Center for Complementary and Alternative Medicine, National Center on Minority Health and Health Disparities, and the National Library of Medicine, among many other institutions. $334,564,000 in appropriations are also made for the research and development of the quality of the medical industry. I really do like this Title of the bill. All of these appropriations seem substantial and warranted.

Title III of HR 3043 appropriates monies to the Department of Education and related administrations. It begins by discussing Education for the Disadvantaged, Impact Aid, School Improvement Programs, Indian Education, Innovation and Improvement, Safe Schools and Citizenship Education, English Language Acquisition, Special Education, Rehabilitation Services and Disability Research. The title then goes on to list a number of 'Special Institutions for Persons with Disabilities.' It also make appropriations for Career, Technical, and Adult Education; Student Financial Assistance, Student Aid Administration, Higher Education, Howard University, College Housing and Academic Facilities Loans Program, Historically Black College and University Capital Financing Program Account, the Institute of Educational Sciences, and Departmental Management. All of these programs seem to be an acceptable use of budgetary funds.

Title IV of HR 3043 make appropriations for related agencies to those discussed previously. These include the Corporation for Public Broadcasting, Federal Mediation and Conciliation Service, National Mediation Board, Occupational Safety and Health Review Commission, Railroad Retirement Board, etc. This is the only section of the document I believe to contain an amount of unnecessary spending.

The recent collapse of companies such as Fannie Mae, Freddie Mac, and AIG illustrate perfectly how poorly the government manages businesses. The federal government was forced to purchase Fannie Mae and Freddie Mac in what could be considered the largest federal bailout in the History of America. Americans, do not be fooled, the Democrats have played a vital role in this ongoing mass government failure including but not limited to: Senator Chris Dodd, Senator John Kerry, Senator Barack Obama, Representative Barney Frank, and many other disloyal, power-hungry members of Congress.

CONGRESS AND PRESIDENT GEORGE W. BUSH

H RES 1258 – "Impeaching George W. Bush, President of the United States, of high crimes and misdemeanors."

This will be consolation to liberals, leftists, moderates, or any other individual that thinks my book contains too much 'personal bias,' as if political literature exists without personal bias, because I absolutely do not want to read the entire impeachment of George W. Bush by the House of Representatives for a number of reasons. 1) I believe this to be an unlawful resolution in light of the fact that Congress authorized the use of military force in Iraq in Concurrent Resolution HJ RES 114 of the 107th Congress, so these Congressional members should also have had the foresight to understand the amount of spending that a war like this would monopolize. The fact that they later revoked this law has no impact on the original document's relevance to the democrats' involvement in the War in Iraq. Just to be clear. 2) I believe it was the Congressmen and women's personal responsibility to obtain as much information about the threat posed by Saddam Hussein and the dictatorial government of Iraq with or without direct legislation by George Bush. He is not their only authority on the subject, nor the only means they have to obtain information. And 3) It simply displeases me to be asked by a proven (later in this Chapter) liar and manipulator Speaker Pelosi to believe that this is anything other than a vain attempt by democrats to skirt their responsibility for voting to authorize military action in Iraq. But there are a multitude of reasons that I need to know and read the information contained in H RES 1258 impeaching the President of the United States so that I can understand the democrats' particular stance on this issue. So here, democrats, I even did the research on this one for you!

I refuse to cite this entire piece of garbage legislation in this book, but I will quote specific excerpts and then describe my views on the rest. If you don't like that format of writing, then go read it yourself.

"In his conduct while President of the United States, George W. Bush, in violation of his constitutional oath to faithfully execute the office of President of the United States and, to the best of his ability, preserve, protect, and defend the Constitution of the United States, and in violation of his constitutional duty under article II, section 3 of the Constitution 'to take care that the laws be faithfully executed', has both personally and acting through his agents and subordinates, together with the Vice President, illegally spent public dollars on a secret propaganda program to manufacture a false cause for war against Iraq.

The Department of Defense (DOD) has engaged in a years-long secret domestic propaganda campaign to promote the invasion and occupation of Iraq. This secret program was defended by the White House Press Secretary following its exposure. This program follows the pattern of crimes detailed in articles I, II, IV, and VIII. The mission of this program placed it within the field controlled by the White House Iraq Group (WHIG), a White House task-force formed in August 2002 to market an invasion of Iraq to the American people. The group included Karl Rove, I. Lewis Libby, Condoleezza Rice, Karen Hughes, Mary Matalin, Stephen Hadley, Nicholas E. Calio, and James R. Wilkinson."

I'm already disgusted to the point of nausea, and I haven't gotten through the entire document yet.

"The WHIG also organized a media blitz in which, between September 7-8, 2002, President Bush and his top advisers appeared on numerous interviews and all provided similarly gripping images about the possibility of nuclear attack by Iraq. The timing was no coincidence, as Andrew Card explained in an interview regarding waiting until after Labor Day to try to sell the American people on military action against Iraq, 'From a marketing point of view, you don't introduce new products in August.'"

This is just hilarity, folks. Do you realize that the Democratic Leadership in Congress – specifically Speaker Pelosi – thinks they have the unabashed authority to criticize media attempts to publicize an advertisement looking at the possibility of the nuclear threat of Iraq. Are the democrats aware that circa November 8, 2002 "The United Nations Security Council…approved a resolution that demand[ed] unfettered access for U.N. inspectors to search for weapons of mass destruction in Iraq"(CNN)? So looking at the nuclear threat of Iraq before the United Nations had even gone in to inspect for weapons of mass destruction in the region would have been a clear concern to Americans at that time. This is the definition of a POLITICAL CAMPAIGN, not a smear campaign. But nice attempt, Speaker Pelosi. No wonder this impeachment never went anywhere substantial.

I am also completely astounded by the Democrats condemnation of 'a secret propaganda program to manufacture a false cause for war against Iraq' since the mainstream media has been manufacturing a cause for Barack Obama for the last six months. My grandfather is a lifelong democrat and war veteran. My mom calls him a 'Ted-Kennedy Democrat;' so you get the picture. My grandfather for the first time in his 85 years of life will be voting for a Republican. He calls Barack Obama "The OB – Out of Bounds" because of the way the mainstream media and liberal agenda has convinced Americans that he cannot be criticized. He is out of bounds territory for Americans to criticize without being raked over the coals for it. And you should all remember that that analogy came straight from a liberal democrat.

Back to this garbage legislation where the House now goes on to define propaganda.

"A March 21, 2005, report by the Congressional Research Service states that 'publicity or propaganda' is defined by the U.S. Government Accountability Office (GAO) to mean either (1) self-aggrandizement by public officials, (2) purely partisan activity, or (3) 'covert propaganda'.

These concerns about 'covert propaganda' were also the basis for the GAO's standard for determining when government-funded video news releases are illegal:

'The failure of an agency to identify itself as the source of a prepackaged news story misleads the viewing public by encouraging the viewing audience to believe that the broadcasting news organization developed the information. The prepackaged news stories are purposefully designed to be indistinguishable from news segments broadcast to the public. When the television viewing public does not know that the stories they watched on television news programs about the government were in fact prepared by the government, the stories are, in this sense, no longer purely factual--the essential fact of attribution is missing.'"

How much propaganda – perhaps not covert, but still propaganda definitely -- do you think the Barack Obama campaign has used during this election? One comes to my mind immediately – "economic justice." Obama's sugary term for socialism. These democrats need to toe the line when they accuse Republicans of using propaganda in any form to fuel a political campaign.

"In all of these actions and decisions, President George W. Bush has acted in a manner contrary to his trust as President and Commander in Chief, and subversive of constitutional government, to the prejudice of the cause of law and justice and to the manifest injury of the people of the United States. Wherefore, President George W. Bush, by such conduct, is guilty of an impeachable offense warranting removal from office."

This is not a rational conclusion. It simply is not. This 'media blitz' the House of Representatives speaks of was warranted as a political campaign. Intelligence had been given to the President and advisors indicating that there MAY BE a nuclear threat in Iraq. Before November 8, 2002, the United Nations had not investigated Iraq for weapons of mass destruction. I believe that is a critical piece of information in understanding why these allegations against George W. Bush are false. I am not disputing that no weapons of mass destruction have been found in Iraq. I am disputing this arrogant resolution put forth by Congress in an attempt to discredit the President of the United States – ignoring the evidence that states that Iraq had not yet been inspected for weapons of mass destruction when this media attention was given to the potential threat posed by an Iraqi nuclear program.

Article II of this bill is titled – "Falsely, Systematically, and With Criminal Intent Conflating the Attacks of September 11, 2001 With Misrepresentation of Iraq as an Imminent Security Threat as Part of Fraudulent Justification for a War of Aggression." Lord, that's a mouthful, Speaker. I can't wait to see how you justify and prove 'criminal intent.' Let's read on. I don't want to summarize this nonsensical rhetoric so I will quote more of it.

"In his conduct while President of the United States, George W. Bush, in violation of his constitutional oath to faithfully execute the office of President of the United States and, to the best of his ability, preserve, protect, and defend the Constitution of the United States, and in violation of his constitutional duty under article II, section 3 of the Constitution `to take care that the laws be faithfully executed', has both personally and acting through his agents and subordinates, together with the Vice President, executed a calculated and wide-ranging strategy to deceive the citizens and Congress of the United States into believing that there was and is a connection between Iraq and Saddam Hussein on the one hand, and the attacks of September 11, 2001, and al Qaeda, on the other hand, so as to falsely justify the use of the United States Armed Forces against the nation of Iraq in a manner that is damaging to the national security interests of the United States, as well as to fraudulently obtain and maintain congressional authorization and funding for the use of such military force against Iraq, thereby interfering with and obstructing Congress's lawful functions of overseeing foreign affairs and declaring war.

The means used to implement this deception were and continue to be, first, allowing, authorizing and sanctioning the manipulation of intelligence analysis by those under his direction and control, including the Vice President and the Vice President's agents, and second, personally making, or causing, authorizing and allowing to be made through highly-placed subordinates, including the President's Chief of Staff, the White House Press Secretary and other White House spokespersons, the Secretaries of State and Defense, the National Security Advisor, and their deputies and spokespersons, false and fraudulent representations to the citizens of the United States and Congress regarding an alleged connection between Saddam Hussein and Iraq, on the one hand, and the September 11th attacks and al Qaeda, on the other hand, that were half-true, literally true but misleading, and/or made without a reasonable basis and with reckless indifference to their truth, as well as omitting to state facts necessary to present an accurate picture of the truth as follows:

(1) On or about September 12, 2001, former terrorism advisor Richard Clarke personally informed the President that neither Saddam

Hussein nor Iraq was responsible for the September 11th attacks. On September 18, Clarke submitted to the President's National Security Adviser Condoleezza Rice a memo he had written in response to George W. Bush's specific request that stated: (1) the case for linking Hussein to the September 11th attacks was weak; (2) only anecdotal evidence linked Hussein to al Qaeda; (3) Osama Bin Laden resented the secularism of Saddam Hussein; and (4) there was no confirmed reporting of Saddam Hussein cooperating with Bin Laden on unconventional weapons.

(2) Ten days after the September 11th attacks the President received a President's Daily Briefing which indicated that the U.S. intelligence community had no evidence linking Saddam Hussein to the September 11th attacks and that there was `scant credible evidence that Iraq had any significant collaborative ties with Al Qaeda'.

(3) In Defense Intelligence Terrorism Summary No. 044-02, issued in February 2002, the United States Defense Intelligence Agency cast significant doubt on the possibility of a Saddam Hussein-al Qaeda conspiracy: `Saddam's regime is intensely secular and is wary of Islamic revolutionary movements. Moreover, Baghdad is unlikely to provide assistance to a group it cannot control.'.

The Democrats in Congress fail to prove the only thing that would validate their argument here, and that is criminal intent. I will show you why:

"Conclusion 1: Statements by the President, Vice President, Secretary of State and the National Security Advisor regarding a possible Iraqi nuclear weapons program were generally substantiated by intelligence community estimates, but did not convey the substantial disagreements that existed in the intelligence community.

Prior to the October 2002 National Intelligence Estimate, some intelligence agencies assessed that the Iraqi government was reconstituting a nuclear weapons program, while others disagreed or expressed doubts about the evidence. The Estimate itself expressed the majority view that the program was being reconstituted, but included clear dissenting views from the State Department's Bureau of Intelligence and Research, which argued that reconstitution was not underway, and the Department of Energy, which argued that aluminum tubes sought by Iraq were probably not intended for a nuclear program."

This conclusion comes from the "Select Committee on Intelligence" of the United States Senate 110th Congress. It is a Report on 'Whether public statements regarding Iraq by U.S. Government Officials were substantiated by intelligence information, together with, additional and minority views.' The document was ordered to be printed April 27, 2007. I would also like to note that this information was given to the Democratic Leadership in Congress in April, and yet they still felt the need to pursue an impeachment of George W. Bush which was not completed until June. They clearly ignored this information and concocted this impeachment legislation without even glancing over it.

More importantly, with the information that there was substantiated intelligence supporting the idea of nuclear weapons in Iraq, then we cannot be convinced that George W. Bush's attempt was not solely for the preservation of the American way of life. They call the George Bush war campaign a propaganda campaign, and that may be true to an extent, but these were valid political campaigns relevant to public concern at the time. The democrats want to demonize and criminalize George W. Bush for actions that their party is openly notorious for.

I suppose I will allow the democrats that there was no Saddam Hussein/al Qaeda conspiracy; however, I do not believe that specific propaganda campaign to be of relevance to our justification to invade Iraq. I have already outlined in the above portions on legislation by Congress on the War in Iraq that I believe the Iraq war is justified on the grounds listed above dealing with Hussein's specific acts of violence committed against his own people and foreign inspectors. Nor did they prove that George W. Bush's intent with the Saddam Hussein conspiracy was criminal. The evidence presented in this amendment does seem to implicate President Bush in telling untruths to the American public. However, I do not think this constitutes a criminal action that warrants removal from office. Especially since former President Bill Clinton perjured himself in a court of law and still retained his seat in office.

H RES 1221 – "Raising a question of the privileges of the House."

The text of the legislation for House Resolution 1221 can be found below. I think it is necessary that the American public read this entire document to fully understand the seriousness and severity of these actions – specifically of Speaker Pelosi and Leader Hoyer.

Whereas the Democratic Leadership has engaged in a continuing pattern of withholding accurate information vital for Members of the House of Representatives to have before voting on legislation;

Whereas the conference report on H.R. 2419, which was adopted by the House on May 14, 2008, and the Senate on May 15, 2008, contained title III, relating to trade, which contained sections 3001 through 3301;

Whereas the Speaker and the Clerk certified that the enrolled copy of H.R. 2419 transmitted to the President was a true and accurate reflection of the actions taken by the House and Senate;

Whereas the enrolled copy certified by the Speaker and the Clerk and presented to the President failed to include title III and sections 3001 through 3301 and was not an accurate or complete document;

Whereas the President vetoed and returned to the House said certified copy;

Whereas before laying the President's message before the House, the Speaker and the Democratic Leadership were informed by the Office of the Law Revision Counsel and the Committee on Agriculture that said certified copy was erroneous and not an accurate or complete document;

Whereas on May 21, 2008, the Democratic Leadership deliberately chose to ignore that notification and instead allowed the House to vote on an incorrect version of this legislation;

Whereas a veto override requires 2/3 of the House to vote in the affirmative, and knowledge of this mistake may have influenced each Member's decision and therefore changed the outcome of this vote, which is why the Democratic Leadership chose not to pursue a correction of this legislation;

Whereas the effect of these actions raises serious constitutional questions and jeopardizes the legal status of this legislation;

Whereas Speaker Pelosi and Majority Leader Hoyer knowingly scheduled and began consideration of the President's veto of H.R. 2419, without regard to the serious and obvious constitutional questions and detrimental implications to the sanctity of the House and its process;

Whereas at the direction of the Republican Leader, senior staff contacted the Chief-of-Staff to the Speaker and the Floor Director for the Majority Leader, requesting that they immediately halt consideration of the veto message until the facts surrounding the errors could be sorted out and all Members could be notified;

Whereas the Democratic Leadership refused that request;

Whereas in the 109th Congress, the current Speaker, Nancy Pelosi, offered a privileged resolution, H. Res. 683, accusing the Republicans of concealment, incompetence, and corruption with respect to the enrollment error of the Deficit Reduction Act;

Whereas the Deficit Reduction Act was the subject of numerous lawsuits questioning its validity due to the enrollment error, including a lawsuit filed by several Democratic Members;

Whereas in a memorandum from the Clerk of the House to Speaker Nancy Pelosi entitled 'Farm Bill Omission' and dated May 21, 2008, the Clerk stated 'Enrolling Division staff expressed concern in receiving direct calls from Leadership and the Committee to accelerate the enrolling process.'; and

Whereas the Democratic Leadership's repeated efforts to thwart the normal legislative process by cutting corners, ignoring requirements of the Constitution and House rules, and rushing through legislation with major errors, forces Members to vote on controversial legislation without thorough time for review and must be denounced: Now, therefore, be it

RESOLVED, THAT--

(1) the Committee on Standards of Official Conduct shall begin an immediate investigation into the abuse of power surrounding the inaccuracies in the process and enrollment of H.R. 2419, Food and Energy Security Act of 2007, vetoed by the President on May 21, 2008; and

(2) the Speaker, Majority Leader and other Members of the Democratic Leadership are hereby admonished for their roles in the events surrounding this enrollment error.

(The Library of Congress)

Let me give a brief summary of the contents of this resolution for clarity, H R 2419 – "Food and Energy Security Act of 2007" was a resolution put forth by the House of Representatives. This document gave a detailed description for distribution of funds to various programs. Speaker Pelosi and Leader Hoyer were informed by two bodies, the Office of the Law Revision Counsel and the Committee on Agriculture, that the document was incomplete and not fit to be presented to the President on those grounds. Speaker Pelosi and Leader Hoyer signed off on the document anyway as being a complete and accurate document. It was presented to President Bush and vetoed. Speaker Pelosi then asked for a 2/3rds override of the presidential veto on this bill, even though she knew from the beginning that the document was inaccurate and incomplete. The 2/3rds override was not successful, and the legislation failed. So H RES 1221 was instituted in order to scold and further admonish these two manipulative scoundrels from ever intentionally perjuring themselves again. I personally call for the criminal trial of Speaker Nancy Pelosi on the grounds of perjury. A signed certificate sent to the President asking for his signature on an incomplete document is one of the most egregious miscarriages of justice I have seen while researching the Democratic Congress, and it should be noted as such. And apparently the withholding of accurate information has become commonplace in Congress. It needs to be put an end to.

Also, I would just like to point out this specific part of the legislation because it is an important repercussion of this scandal to understand: "*Whereas the effect of these actions raises serious constitutional questions and jeopardizes the legal status of this legislation.*"

So I decided to research this a bit further. I wanted to know exactly which part of this "Food and Energy Security Act of 2007" **(H RES 2419)** Nancy Pelosi felt the individual right to leave out of this inaccurate bill she then signed off on to present to the President of the United States. Title III of this article encompasses the "Food for Peace" initiatives in reference to trade. Yes, my fellow Americans, Nancy Pelosi and the Clerk thought they could be sneaky and put provisions in the budget for 2009 allowing *to:*

"ensure, to the maximum extent practicable, that options for providing food aid for emergency and nonemergency needs shall not be subject to limitation, including in-kind commodities, provision of funds for agricultural commodity procurement, and monetization of commodities, on the condition that the provision of those commodities or funds – (i) is based on the assessments of need and intended to benefit the food security

of, or otherwise assist, recipients, and (ii) is provided in a manner that avoids disincentives to local agricultural production and marketing and with minimal potential for disruption of commercial markets"(H RES 2419 Sec. 3003)

This is just one portion of Title III that was conveniently left out of the President's copy of this bill. In Section 3008 of this same Title – also left out of the complete document – provisions are made for the fiscal year of 2009 to appropriate a portion of the budget: *'(A) to assess the types and quality of agricultural commodities and products donated for food aid; (B) to adjust products and formulations (including the potentital introduction of new fortificants and products) as necessary to cost-effectively meet nutrient needs of target populations; and (C) to test prototypes'* (Subsection (h) of revised document or H RES 2419 Sec. 3008). So let me get this straight, Pelosi, you and the other Democratic nitwits in Congress slyly attempted to inject appropriations into our 2009 budget to not only give food to ANY other country for emergency or NONEMERGENCY needs, in fact, let me quote the exact wording again, *"options for providing food aid for emergency and nonemergency needs shall not be subject to limitation."* So you have not only obligated the United States to donate our necessary food supply to other countries, but you have even extended this courtesy to include NONEMERGENCY NEEDS? Have you lost it altogether, Nancy Pelosi? Do you realize the effects of rising food costs IN THIS COUNTRY? We do not need provisions obligating Americans to ship our food overseas, one of the few remaining American industries the government has not thus far crippled. Thank you, Democrats, for making a thorough, yet not so clever attempt to appropriate one of our top export industries to GIVE our food to neighboring countries or those you deem to be suffering. This bill gives the President the discretion to decide when the countries are in 'need,' I suppose; however, there is one person running for the President of the United States in 2008 that I simply do not trust with the authority to distribute our crops overseas. Let's be clear, I'm talking about Barack Obama.

Additionally, have the democrats not been whining and complaining about the deficit? Of course they have, but they allow for 'monetization of commodities' in this bill to be distributed to countries in 'distress' or some mumbo jumbo. I am so sick of hearing the democrats endlessly rant about the trillions of dollars of debt in this country, and yet they have no problem 'monetizing commodities' just to ship them back overseas. So now we're borrowing money from overseas to ship it back overseas. Good plan, democrats.

Nancy Pelosi intentionally left out a Title of a bill containing 30 different sections in an attempt to fool the President of the United States. Unfortunately, it backfired for Nancy Pelosi – but, then again, I have never believed the liberal jargon pinning President Bush as a 'moron' – not for long anyway. The man went to Yale, arguably a better school than Harvard. Just because President Bush doesn't feel the need to use the phrases 'this is our moment' or 'economic justice' 12 times in a speech (of course, most of Barack Obama's vocabulary is meant to intimidate the American public – not inform them) does not mean that he cannot be somewhat effective in noticing a cheating, lying scoundrel speaking for the House of Representatives trying to conceal an unnecessary earmark right under his nose. George got you that time, Pelosi. And you were admonished by the courts for it. That puts a smile on my face.

But the important thing is that people know these facts. These are the kind of things you will not hear talked about by the mainstream media. This would not help their agenda at all so they simply will not report on it. But other Americans can still access the voting records, at least we can right now. There's no telling how many rights Barack Obama will revoke from us, though. It's a troubling thought.

CONCLUSIONS:

In the words of Rush Limbaugh, "[the Democrats] find a scapegoat, then raise taxes." It's a simple yet glaringly true statement. I have proven throughout the course of this Chapter that the Democrats have repeatedly and with intent misled the American public to believe certain things relevant to their political agenda. They have skirted their obligations to addressing concerns plaguing Americans, and they have not been forthright or truthful in their excessive amount of spending on earmarks and legislation intended to fund the environmentalist or socialist causes. This Democratic Congress should be given very little credibility for solving any issue relevant to most Americans. This is a politically correct, but still politically charged Democratic leadership that has thwarted countless Republican attempts for bi-partisan legislation. The legislators most directly involved with the covert attempts to conceal earmarks and direct pieces of legislation should be voted out of office in the next election. If it is time for the American public to render a verdict on the effectiveness of the Democratic Congress, then we should render them guilty of many acts that have hindered progress and development of critical industries of vital importance to the American market.

Chapter Seven

Hillary Rodham Clinton

I'm not going to talk long about Hillary Clinton because she's not in the race anymore and she caved like a coward under the pressure of Barack Obama and the Democratic Party. I supported a Hillary Clinton Presidency when she was running against Barack Obama in the Primaries because I thought that Hillary Clinton had good alternatives and solutions to the economy and specific economic concerns that I believe are of vital importance. However, she has thoroughly disappointed me as a politician and a woman because she allowed her party to dictate to her how she should act after she lost the race. She fought hard while the race was going on, but she did not stick to her ideals once it was clear that the Democratic Party wanted Barack Obama to be the nominee – which I still, to this day, do not understand. I believe that Hillary Clinton is sticking to her word when she said that she would support a Barack Obama nomination if that were to be the case, but I do not respect her support of a man who is contrary to many of the ideals that Americans live by every day. Barack Obama is contrary to many of the beliefs that Hillary Clinton values, and she may be putting those aside for the sake of the election, but she is also putting aside values that many Americans will not just as whimsically throw away. If Hillary Clinton truly has the good of the American public at heart, then she will stop this unnecessary support of Barack Obama, and, even secretly, vote for John McCain. If Hillary Clinton wants to be elected at some point in the future, then she needs to show that she is a woman that will stand by her word and her beliefs no matter the scrutiny they may endure. I'm not sure why the Democrats have not figured out that this is the reason they cannot get elected in the United States of America, but it is because to be President of this country an individual must be so dedicated to their beliefs that they will stand beside them, shout them from the rooftops, intelligently debate with anyone that opposes their views, and defeat all opposition that comes their way. A candidate must make sure to represent the well being of the American public in their actions, and if you are inconsistent in your beliefs and your convictions, then you do not represent the American public.

I want anyone who voted for or supported Hillary Clinton while she was running in the primaries to remember one very important thing about that nomination process though: What happened to Florida and Michigan? Why did they only get half of their representatives? I wonder...

I guess the popular vote is not so important to Barack Obama after all.

Chapter Eight

Gas Prices

Americans love to drive. They love to drive their automobiles, motorcycles, scooters, etc. My boyfriend and I even saw a scooter with training wheels the other day riding through the mountains for a nice summer drive. Americans love automobiles, and we should – as we played a critical role in their assimilation into mainstream society. Henry Ford invented the assembly line in 1913 and a functioning transmission, both of which propelled automobile sales exponentially (Crandall). He made cars affordable to average Americans. We are proud of these inventions, these innovations that were uniquely American at birth. So why when we are so proud of our achievements are we now being fed lies by the Democratic Party that would lead us to believe that the climate changes are due to our unnecessary use of these automobiles? Among other factors that extremist liberals say contribute to global warming and other environmental problems, the democratic legislators would like Americans to believe that our use of gasoline has deteriorated the environment to the point of decay. This is simply an untrue statement. The effects of smog and emissions by automobiles are by no means good, but they are more harmful to us as individuals than to the environment as a whole.

But back to the major concern facing Americans today – gas prices. How can our legislators and government officials help to drive down gas prices? This is the main concern. Americans obviously know that our legislators have the ability to place regulations on trade to limit the buying and buying back of barrels of oil which leads to inflated gas prices, but they have not put any measures in place yet. We have oil reserves, we have bastions that could be drilled in for new oil discoveries. Yet we must let them fester because liberals do not want to taint the mosquito population in Alaska. This is not a joke. The Democratic Party will not allow offshore drilling or expansion in ANWR or the OCS and has blocked countless Republican attempts to pass legislation regarding oil expansion (more on this topic in 'The Democratic Congress'). America has the resources inside of herself to mend our gas crisis. It may not take gas down to single digit dollar signs, but gas prices would be decreased SUBSTANTIALLY by drilling offshore. That fact cannot really be disputed as we would have more oil that would not have to be imported. American oil. The Energy Information Administration states that "two countries exported more than 1.50 million barrels [of oil] per day to the United States." These two countries are Canada and Saudi Arabia. The solution to gas prices is to drive down the cost of exports by creating a substantial oil market in the United States. We cannot compete with the costs of importing crude oil from other countries such as Venezuela, Nigeria, Iraq, Angola, Algeria, Brazil, and Kuwait. We will never be able to compete with these countries until we form a functional oil market in the United States.

President George W. Bush met with an economic team of advisors to discuss offshore drilling (U.S. Department of Energy). He had this to say about solving the gas crisis, "The problem, of course, is that gasoline prices are up, which has affected the people here in our country. And one of the main reasons why gasoline prices are up is because crude oil prices are up. And one reason crude oil prices are up is because demand is outstripping supply. And therefore, what can we do about it? And that ought to be the question the United States Congress asks. And one way to deal with supply problems is to increase supply here in America." YES! We have been waiting for the President to come up with a solution to this crisis, and then he presents a bill that would promote offshore drilling and expansion. The Democratic

Congress will not let this bill pass. The Democratic Congress standing in the way of finding real solutions to the economic problems we're facing? I wouldn't see it happening any other way. But what are the motivations for these politicians to ignore these outrageously high gas prices? Well, Barack Obama's only problem with the inflated gas prices is that "they went up so quickly." That doesn't sound like a man with a solution to me. That sounds like a man satisfied with the outcome of a situation that really has nothing more to say on the topic other than a quick breeze-over that will get him a small amount of media coverage. He would only want a small amount of media coverage on that though since he has no solution, and that is what Americans are looking for. But let's be even more clear about it, he does not want a solution. His Marxist mindset has led him to believe that regulations on our oil companies and extensive intervention by the government will be much more solace to the American public than a solution to the gas crisis. Barack Obama is more out of touch with me, as a Southern white woman than I have ever experienced. Especially from a politician who thinks he has the experience and foresight to manage the Greatest Country in the world. He does not have either of these things. Americans, every single American, black, white, Hispanic, Taiwanese, etc., need to realize this and take charge of this situation. We must not vote in a man that does not understand the very ideals and principles that America was founded upon.

John McCain would like to institute a gas tax holiday at some point in the near future. Democrats and extremist liberals balk at this idea screaming that the economists see no long-term solution to the crisis with a gas tax holiday. Well, gee, I could never have figured that one out for myself. This gas tax holiday is not meant to be a long-run solution. The long-run solution is offshore drilling. The Democrats have ABSOLUTELY NO SOLUTION AT ALL. And I am absolutely sick of being lectured by these dense individuals who have very little grasp of the economy at all, touting that this gas tax holiday cannot be a REAL solution to our gas problem. Opponents to the gas tax holiday: Just sit down and shut up, Americans at the gas pump would appreciate a gas tax holiday. Specifically those Americans that drive SUV's, HEMI trucks, and 18-wheelers. And you can stay seated on this topic until you find a solution, until then, keep your mouth closed about it and listen to the more intelligent people discuss an actual solution.

The problem with extremist liberals and Democratic politicians is that they simply do not care about gas prices. They use mass transportation or have so much money shooting out of their rear-ends (cough: John Edwards, Al Gore, Pelosi) that they can afford egregiously high prices. Well, as an average middle-class American, I cannot afford these gas prices, and public transportation is NOT AN OPTION in this area. I know, leftists, imagine that, a world where we have to drive cars to get places, and all of our resources and food are also imported via automobiles or airplanes that use gasoline.

Aside from gas prices affecting how much we spend everyday at the gas pump, crude oil prices affect our lives in many other ways. Airline prices are higher than I have ever witnessed. The men and women driving 18-wheelers for a living (transporting our necessary goods) are in disarray. They cannot afford these gas prices because many truckers must pay the gas expenses out of pocket. Think of the cost that diesel gas has risen to and then ask yourself how much money these drivers are putting into an 18-wheeler just for one trip to deliver goods. Gas prices will also affect the boating industry and other transportation industries (including taxi services). Gas prices will also affect our police force since they must drive large, steel, American-made automobiles to ensure our safety everyday. The effects of gas prices on our lives make it clear that gasoline is an inelastic good to most Americans. An inelastic good basically refers to an immediate necessity, but it technically means that the price of the good is 'inelastic' in that an increase in price will cause a dramatic or noticeable fall in demand for the good. (This concept is discussed at length in the Chapter on Ideologies, the section about Capitalism.)

NPR reports that "Offshore drilling has also turned into an election-year issue, with presumptive Republican presidential candidate John McCain supporting ending the drilling ban, while the campaign of presumptive Democratic nominee Barack Obama says opening up offshore drilling 'would merely prolong the failed energy policies we have seen from Washington for 30 years.'" Another beautiful sentiment from Barack Obama on our oil crisis. I want to know what this man proposes as a solution. I do not ever want to hear him talk about our "failed energy policies" when he has proposed NO

SOLUTION. Why do people ignore his arrogance day in and day out? He is the most arrogant, pretentious, over-inflated piece of ivy-league trash that we have seen walking in Washington in the last 30 years. His education and extensive vocabulary does not give him the credibility or foresight to deal with the issues being presented to him. This is why he proposes no solution. He has no solution nor does he intend to spend his precious time trying to come up with a solution. He spends his time gallivanting overseas with Iraqi Prime Minister Nuri al-Maliki or German citizens (Kulish).

The democrats are extremely inefficient when it comes to energy exploration and preservation. Barack Obama said that he does not support drilling in ANWR because it would still leave an oil deficit. He clearly does not care if the government's money – taxes – are not revoked, as suggested with John McCain's gas tax holiday; his agenda can only be achieved if he continues to demonize Exxon as the real culprit of the oil crisis. Exxon is not the culprit of the oil crisis. That is simply not factual, but I don't hear the mainstream media making a grand spectacle because Barack Obama is making blatant false statements to the American public. Exxon facilitates the development of gasoline through crude oil imports then manufactures the product and efficiently delivers it to the American public day in and day out. The oil industry is very well-maintained and functions very well in the context of the American marketplace. Without companies like Exxon to produce and distribute gasoline to gas pumps, we would not be able to utilize the millions of barrels of crude oil a day that we are importing from various foreign countries – again, the top 2 crude oil import countries are Canada and Saudi Arabia. The fact that Exxon makes a profit should show the American public that they are doing an excellent job providing their product to the American public – as many Americans are spending their money at the million or so Exxon-Mobile gas stations countrywide. Do not demonize Exxon because that mindset only leads to further misunderstandings about the real situation we are in with a lack of crude oil in America. Exxon does quite a bit more in relation to the production of oil than the foreign countries importing crude oil do – and they are the ones that have been making most of the profit from this oil crisis as they are buying and buying back barrels of oil before they are shipping it to the United States. Foreign countries cost-efficiently drill for crude oil (as we could do in America), but

Exxon and other gas companies manufacture the crude oil to make it available and useful to Americans. I am sick of hearing Democrats or uninformed leftists and liberals complain about how George Bush is "in with the big oil companies." Of course he is because he's not an idiot. He understands the importance and significance of American oil companies in the day-to-day lives of Americans. He understands that this is an inelastic good to Americans, and he wants to ensure that Exxon will indefinitely keep producing gasoline for Americans as long as we need it to move automobiles, airplanes, or other modes of transportation from one place to the other. It really is not a difficult concept to grasp. It is just rarely exposed truthfully. I'm sure there are other motivations for George Bush to be polite and somewhat generous to the oil companies, but the reasoning I just explained should quell the fear that George Bush is doing it 'for money.' Please, that's just not realistic. He's doing it for America. He does not need any more money, and he is not a power-hungry man, no matter the lengths that Communists and leftists will go to accuse him of such.

George W. Bush has been a great leader during times of terror. He has not always made the right decision; I'm sure even he would admit that. But he has done the best that he could do in the adversarial political climate that he was in. I know my vote for him in 2004 was well spent. I think he is a man that stands by his word and looks out for the best intentions of this country. He is not a perfect man; there is no perfect man. But he has done a fine job as President leading this country during a time of terror, a time of war, and now a time of complete mismanagement by Congress. History will recall President Bush as a man of his word – no matter the lengths that Democrats go to demean his character. I will always think of George Bush as a kind and generous man – not always with the best solutions, but always with the best intentions for this country. And that is how I want to remember all of my American presidents. Everyone has faults, but only the strongest of men can admit to those and take responsibility for their actions. George Bush takes responsibility for himself and his administration and for the state this country is in right now. Hence why George Bush has come up with an actual solution to the gas crisis, and the democrats have not. And that is ironic since the Democrats should be the ones taking responsibility for the gas crisis since as Americans can recall, we did not see these egregious prices until the

Democratic Leadership was voted into Congress. But why would they want to bring prices down when they enjoy them being up?

Every leftist democrat opposes coming down on prices for fuel, but they promote solar and wind energy, as if that has yielded any sort of real outcome at all in the past few years. Wind and solar energy in decades may be useful to everyday Americans, but the technology has not been developed yet. Investing in solar or wind-powered energy is much less practical than investing in oil, which we know we can utilize for American industries, RIGHT NOW to help adjust prices in the market. I will only be giving credit to the T. Boone Pickins Plan (pickinsplan.com) in this book because I think investing in wind energy is necessary, but that does not mean we should allow the American public to suffer right now. We are suffering right now because of these prices, and we have the resources to bring these prices down ourselves. Why would we not do that?! Barack Obama has no concrete reasoning behind his stance on drilling offshore since it is believed that even the majority of Californians support drilling offshore now. What should we do since demand for crude oil is outstripping supply in this country? What is the LOGICAL solution to a problem of this sort? Increase supply. It is the only logical alternative at this juncture.

I have to talk further about the democrats blatantly skirting their obligations to the American public by adjourning Congress until September without even discussing the issue of our crude oil crisis. What is this garbage? I understand that Nancy 'stretch' Pelosi (Levin) and Harry 'spineless' Reid may not have any major concern with $4.00+ per gallon gas prices, but the American people DO have a concern. You were elected by members of your state to represent them as best you can. You are to discuss issues of relevance to your constituents. You are not to use your own agendas to create more economic concerns for the American people. YOU are an economic concern to the American people, Nancy Pelosi, and you, Harry Reid. I'm slightly disappointed that George Bush did not reconvene them to Congress regardless of their vote, and let's not forget that this vote was almost sung in unison by every democrat in the House of Representatives with 'Stretch' Pelosi leading the tune. What happened to bi-partisanship? Didn't the democrats tout that during the elections of 2006 as a major selling point to their campaigns? Yet another lie by the democratic party to fool the ignorant into believing that they actually had somewhat decent intentions for individual American citizens, but that has simply shown not to be the case. If I find out that any of my legislators at the state and federal level in Tennessee ever become involved in this blocking of oil production, they will have a vehement letter of protest waiting for them when they return home. (Bredesen, I'm watching you.) And, trust me, they know how the voters in my state feel about it, and I can't see any of them turning their backs on the current oil crisis for political expediency. Although Bob Corker's name is on a bi-partisan piece of legislation that I heard promotes but severely restricts oil discoveries. Bob Corker, so help me, you will have a letter of protest on your desk if I find out that this piece of legislation is trash. It had better be more lenient to oil drilling than I heard.

Here is a quotation from Barack Obama on the oil crisis, "John McCain's gas tax holiday was really more psychological for people. This country doesn't need another Dr. Phil we need someone to SOLVE the Economy…" Wait one second Barack Obama, if we need someone to 'solve' the Economy, then you are definitely not the man for the job. Let's get that straight from the start. Second, a national gas tax holiday, as I have previously stated, would be beneficial to every single American in this country – this is indisputable since we would all be spending less of our money (not to mention less money for the transportation and shipment of our goods across the country and around the globe) at the gas pumps. But this is just another example of how out of touch Barack Obama is with the real concerns of the American public. Americans want to know that our government will do something about this gas crisis, but all presidential hopeful Barack Obama can do is mock our troubles saying we should just 'fill up [our] tires with air and get a tune-up.' There are a number of obscenities I would like to scream at Barack Obama for making an asinine comment such as that when we are facing a real threat to our internal security – this man's lack of knowledge or understanding of the oil industry in this country. The oil industry is instrumental for economic prosperity and growth. I have heard so many people complaining that Exxon made a couple billion dollar profit this quarter. Why do people insist on complaining every time American companies excel – or not even excel, Exxon just hasn't crumbled under the mental recession the media has us in right now. Exxon can make a profit, and guess what Americans, that is GOOD for you. Do you want the Economy to fail? Because rooting for the oil industry and other top industries in this country to fail is rooting for the American Economy to fail. It really is that simple. Without these companies' stability and job opportunities, the market in this country will plummet.

And what is this nonsense about bringing all of the speed limits in the country down to 55 miles per hour? Why are we slowing ourselves down in America when we should be innovating to become MORE efficient, not less efficient? I am appalled that this is viewed as some kind of solution to the gas crisis. We are innovating to create cars, the Ferrari Enzo registers 217+ miles per hour and can go 0-60 in 3.4 seconds, and the Porsche Carrera GT that can hit 0-60 in 3.9 seconds (Fastest Cars). Not if they change the speed limits in all our states. We can't even utilize the vast amount of technology that we and other countries are gaining because of these kinds of policies. Additionally, it absolutely is not the authority of the federal government to dictate what the speed limits in specific states are. This is a right of the STATES to choose all on their own. Mostly because, astonishingly enough, they know the roads in their specific state better than the democrats in Congress do. It's just outrageous that they're already proposing solutions to begin controlling people's everyday lives, and some Americans are standing by and twiddling their thumbs – brainwashed by an ideologue with little credibility and no realistic solutions.

Liberals, leftists, and those with ill-intent toward the United States living in other countries, are just incensed and obsessed with the American dependence on oil. Why is this such a difficult concept for these people to grasp? In the United States in 2008, gasoline, specifically crude oil, is an inelastic good, a necessity that Americans cannot live without. What is so fascinating about this fact? Yes. We need oil and petroleum to move vehicles from one place to another so we can continue to be an efficient nation. These people are just ridiculous when they assert that we are the most wasteful nation in the world (NYT) simply because we use so much oil. I classify most of the democratic Congress wasteful – simply on the basis of their lavish existence (and the numerous pieces of useless legislation I poured over in order to write this book), so I suppose that will be just fine to hear them call Americans wasteful because of our dependence on oil. I don't know if these other countries and the democrats want applause for being able to identify an inelastic good, but I'm not applauding that they figured it out and are now attempting to hamper any effort to bring the price down to a rate that is reasonable for most Americans. My boyfriend had the idea that if they are going to make the speed limit 55 then it should be a flat speed limit, so to speak, and every driver should have the discretion to drive up to 55 miles per hour on any road. I wouldn't be opposed to that, but somehow I still know that the democrats would cry injustice. They don't want the American people to have the discretion to make personal choices. They have shown that with their actions. (Reference the section on the Democratic Congress and Energy Efficiency.)

I've heard it rumored today that Barack Obama is planning to shift his position on offshore drilling. He said we could save the same amount of oil that we would get from drilling in ANWR by 'filling your tires up with air and getting a tune-up.' When was the last time that Barack Obama drove a car all on his own without being chauffeured around or flown around on his "Barack Obama One" jet or whatever it's called? My car doesn't get a tune-up, Senator Obama, it gets an oil change.

Here are some more Barack Obama quotations I heard mostly on the Sean Hannity show:

'You could inflate your tires up to the proper level, then we would save all the money that he wants to get off of drilling.'

Americans, please go inflate all of your tires if they are unnecessarily low. This is a good piece of automotive advice; however, it will not end the U.S. dependency on foreign oil. It is actually a slight insult to the American public to assume that they cannot properly assess the amount of air in their own tires and inflate them when necessary. My car even has an indicator light when the tires get low (look at that innovation, Senator), so this bit of outdated advice from Senator Barack Obama doesn't really help me at all with $4.00+ gallon gas prices. However, Senator Barack Obama is most concerned that he's being made fun of by conservative pundits for making the suggestion at all. He had this to say, "they're making fun of a step that every expert says would absolutely reduce our oil consumption" No, Mr. Obama, they are making fun of your inept attempt to quell the economic concern of rising oil prices by suggesting that the American public inflate their tires. That will be just fine, we will all go inflate our tires, what now? What will you do now to ensure that gas prices go down? Americans will do our part in this and inflate our tires, but you, Senator Obama, should make a similar commitment to the American public that ensures that you will aid and help our citizens by decreasing the cost of fuel by increasing American supply of crude oil and allowing drilling in ANWR. If Senator Obama can make that commitment to Americans, then we can certainly all make a commitment to keeping our tires properly inflated. So then all parties will be happy, right Senator Obama?

However, I just don't see that line of reasoning appealing to Senator Obama because he continues to insult conservatives and the Republican movement who mocked his bit of advice, exclaiming that "[i]t's like these guys take pride in being ignorant!" No, Barack, you take pride in completely ignoring or whimsically sweeping over any issue of immediate or direct relevance to the American public. That is what they're mocking. Just for clarity.

CONCLUSIONS:

In 2008, Americans are dependent on crude oil to function their day-to-day lives. This fact requires immediate intervention by the federal government allowing for American oil discoveries to be made in ANWR and the OCS. If we do not make this critical step in the production and distribution of crude oil, a commodity which Americans cannot live without until a substantial advancement in energy-refining technology is pioneered then the economy will recede indefinitely. Steps and precautions are taken to preserve the wildlife and surrounding ecosystems, and these methods are effective. We must be concerned with the immediate needs of the American public, and we need gas prices to come down. We do not need to live in fear of not being able to transport ourselves to work because we cannot afford the fuel prices. We should still be able to drive cars at our own leisure, but we will take necessary precautions and invest in innovative industries that will eliminate the need for gasoline-powered automobiles, airplanes, and other transportation units. However, that theory cannot substantiate the American public right now. We must drill for oil. We must not inhibit the resourceful and efficient production of a good that we cannot live without. I am confident that our Congressmen will fight hard enough to pass legislation that will effectively alleviate some of our economic concerns with rising oil prices; however, I will remain vigilant to any new developments in energy development and exploration, and I will also remain aware of those who thwart or prohibit oil discovery and refining because those are the individuals who cannot look to the greater good of Americans but must use their own agenda to put forth legislation contrary to the American public's agenda.

Chapter Nine

The Wars in Iraq and Afghanistan

"When I am this party's nominee, my opponent will not be able to say that I voted for the war in Iraq; or that I gave George Bush the benefit of the doubt on Iran; or that I supported Bush-Cheney policies of not talking to leaders that we don't like. And he will not be able to say that I wavered on something as fundamental as whether or not it is ok for America to torture — because it is never ok... I will end the war in Iraq... I will close Guantanamo. I will restore habeas corpus. I will finish the fight against Al Qaeda. And I will lead the world to combat the common threats of the 21st century: nuclear weapons and terrorism; climate change and poverty; genocide and disease. And I will send once more a message to those yearning faces beyond our shores that says, "You matter to us. Your future is our future. And our moment is now." – Barack Obama, Des Moines, Iowa, November 10, 2007.

Remember the growing threat of Iran, Americans.

Russia has now invaded their own sovereign territory – Georgia -- and has caused chaos and ruin in the region. The United States will not be sending ground troops in to support Georgia, but our continued allegiance should be to Georgia's freedom as its own territory from the corruption of the Russian government run by Czar Putin.

Nothing can begin this section of the book better than a brief recap of the effect that the terrorist attacks on September 11, 2001 had on the American people. On September 11, Americans began their days as usual, little did we know what was looming in our futures. We were about to witness the most heinous tragedy that people of my generation have ever witnessed. And we were not only going to know that this tragedy occurred, we watched it on repeat countless times. We saw the videos of those misguided planes driven by terror into our Twin Towers in lower Manhattan, New York City. We endured this. We lived through this. We felt the pain of knowing that the lives of our citizens had now been threatened by a foreign invader. And worse. One we could not pinpoint precisely. The lives of New Yorkers were shaken to the very core. Would they know someone that had been a part of this horrific tragedy? Worse, would it be one of their own family members? I cannot imagine what it was like to be a New Yorker on September 11, but I do think that the New Yorkers endured that attack with dignity and a valiance I would expect only from my fellow Americans. Regardless of the fact that Rudy Giuliani did not succeed in this Presidential race, he still has my respect and gratitude for being "America's Mayor" in a time when Americans needed leadership the most. But the one person who deserves the most praise for his presence on 9/11/01 is President George W. Bush. Give credit where credit is due. George Bush was our beacon of hope during these attacks. George Bush may not be an eloquent public speaker, but he had my family and I in tears with his strength, courage, and natural perseverance. He had a breathtaking strength about him that day. These were his words. Keep in mind they do not mirror the resolve in his face or the determination in his voice.

"Good evening. Today, our fellow citizens, our way of life, our very freedom came under attack in a series of deliberate and deadly terrorist acts. The victims were in airplanes, or in their offices; secretaries, businessmen and women, military and federal workers; moms and dads, friends and neighbors. Thousands of lives were suddenly ended by evil, despicable acts of terror.

The pictures of airplanes flying into buildings, fires burning, huge structures collapsing, have filled us with disbelief, terrible sadness, and a quiet, unyielding anger. These acts of mass murder were intended to frighten our nation into chaos and retreat. But they have failed; our country is strong.

A great people has been moved to defend a great nation. Terrorist attacks can shake the foundations of our biggest buildings, but they cannot touch the foundation of America. These acts shattered steel, but they cannot dent the steel of American resolve.

America was targeted for attack because we're the brightest beacon for freedom and opportunity in the world. And no one will keep that light from shining.

Today, our nation saw evil, the very worst of human nature. And we responded with the best of America -- with the daring of our rescue workers, with the caring for strangers and neighbors who came to give blood and help in any way they could."

But then a strange thing happened to the American people in the wake of September 11, we became strengthened with a newfound resolve that could not be diminished by any man or woman of any nation, creed or belief system. Americans stood united together against the threats posed by these Islamic terrorists. At this point, 9/11 became the driving force behind the ensuing wars against Iraq and Afghanistan. We found out that the culprits behind these attacks were Muslim Extremists – Islamic Terrorists if you will. I recently heard that we are no longer permitted to use the phrases 'Muslim Extremist' and 'Islamic Terrorist.' Here is something you need to learn, Democrats: freedom of speech encompasses all speech that does not pose an imminent threat or danger, even speech that you do not agree with. And I will never refer to the evil minions that caused so much peril and devastation in New York City on that sad day anything other than Islamic Terrorists and Muslim Extremists. That is what they were, and they will not be given the respect to be referred to as anything other than disgusting souls so consumed with their Allah and their all-knowing religion, that they were willing to sacrifice their own lives along with a total of 2,726 American lives for their cause (CDC). These people were cowards, hiding behind a book – faith in a religion that taught them the slogan 'death to America.' I hate these people. With every fiber of my being, I hate the terrorists that attacked America that day. I hate the ones that plan to attack America in the future. But more than that, I hate the people that have stood in the way of American progress for the sake of fundamentalist pacifist principles. Disagreeing with American foreign policy is natural, inevitable even, but standing in the way of our continued military progress (Cindy Sheehan is coming to mind), you have committed treason against your country and in the days of our founding, you would have been hung for it.

We cannot forget the pain and devastation of the September 11, 2001 terrorist attacks committed against the United States. The terrorists are counting on Americans to forget these heinous acts and allow our security to be weakened. Because with a weakening security and alertness comes the dissolve of the resolve the American public has to fight against terrorism. They are counting on our weakness, so we will show none. The difference between the United States of America and countries such as Iraq and Afghanistan is the weakness of any government that has an absence of appropriate checks and balances – a dictatorship or Communist regime, for example. Capitalism and democracy give Americans the resolve to know that our government cannot be corrupted by one body without the interference of the many other bodies of government. Dictatorships and Communist regimes appropriate control to a small portion of leaders who essentially decide the fate of every single citizen on critical decisions such as where to obtain healthcare and many other institutions that we as Americans have the free will to decide all on our own. The people of Iraq and Afghanistan were at the mercy of their government, but Americans control the United States government. We must continue to control our own government. When government controls the people, it can only lead to chaos and despair, especially in a country where individual freedom is valued over handouts and welfare checks.

So the wars begin.

I was unsure how to begin detailing our continued military presence in Iraq and Afghanistan. I will first present you with a quotation from a letter written to Congress by the Honorable Dennis J Hastert Speaker of the House of Representatives, on September 17, 2003:

"Two years ago, we responded to attacks on America by launching a global war against terrorism that has removed gathering threats to America and our allies and has liberated the Iraqi and Afghan people from oppression and fear.

America is making steady progress in the war on terror. Nearly two-thirds of al Qaeda's leadership has been captured or killed.

In Afghanistan, we removed the Taliban from power and shut down terrorist training camps. In Iraq, we led a coalition that removed a dangerous tyrant who sponsored terror, possessed and used weapons of mass destruction, and for 12 years defied the clear demands of the United Nations Security Council. Today, I am submitting a request for 2004 supplemental appropriations for ongoing military and intelligence operations in Iraq, Afghanistan, and elsewhere. Our men and women in uniform, alongside our coalition partners, are bringing peace and stability to Iraq and fighting the terrorist threat. In Afghanistan, our Armed Forces continue to track down terrorists and provide security as the Afghan people rebuild their nation. Our commitment to ongoing operations against terrorism is worthy of our country and critical to our security."

And now it is 2008. America is still dealing with the repercussions of entering into this war despite constant protesting and criticism from pacifists, zealots, neighboring countries, and the United Nations. The UN had sanctioned Iraq on numerous occasions pleading for fair treatment of the citizens and an end to the oppression in the region. I will now quote the United Nations – Economic and Social Council on Commission on Human Rights: (From the sub-commission on Prevention of Discrimination and Protection of Minorities, Forty-third session) "Agenda Item 6: Question of the violation of human rights and fundamental freedoms, including policies of racial discrimination and segregation and of apartheid, in all countries, with particular report of the Sub-Commission established under Commission on Human Rights resolution 8 (XXIII)…" However, the United Nations has been outspoken in their protest of the American invasion of Iraq to correct the injustices that Iraqis – Saddam Hussein specifically – were committing against their own people. Saddam Hussein after being sanctioned countless times by the UN and other legislative bodies would not rectify his horrific methods of murder, mutilation, and mass slaughter (on his own citizens and others in the Middle East) so the United States brought an end to his regime as dictator. Saddam Hussein was removed from his leadership position in Iraq and later executed after convicted by courts of heinous human rights violations. Countless human rights violations. American Soldiers, Marines, Airmen, and Seamen were dispersed to the Middle East to ensure that Iraq could never pose a threat to the United States of America or their own citizens again. We later were informed during the progression of the wars that the Iraqi government under Saddam Hussein did not directly facilitate or have involvement in the September 11, 2001 terrorist attacks; however, the reasons were present even without direct involvement to invade and free that nation. That is clearly up for debate and speculation, but from the information I have seen, the numerous UN treaties, sanctions, and resolutions concerning Iraq's heinous treatment of their citizens, I am convinced that the United States was justified in entering into the War in Iraq. It is always a difficult thing to find enough justification for entering into a war since it inevitably means justifying killing – sometimes of innocent civilians. I understand the pacifist argument; however, those of us who think this war was justified (it kills the Democrats to admit that it was a substantial number of them in the beginning – including Hillary Clinton) understand that we are not justifying unnecessary killing, we are justifying military action in order to preserve, repair, or completely reassemble another government. And we are justified to enter into this country committing these egregious acts on the principle of freedom. The Iraqi people deserved a nation where they do not have to fear their government, as we Americans do not fear ours. Civilian casualty statistics in Iraq have ranged from 30,000 by an optimistic George W. Bush to 655,000 done by an independent study. However, General George W. Casey, the top American military commander in Iraq had this to say about that study, " That 650,000 number seems way, way beyond any number that I have seen. I've not seen a number higher than 50,000. And so I don't give it that much credibility at all." (CNN transcript)

And I want to make sure it's clear that I'm not claiming to be an expert on foreign policy. I trust the generals, commanders, and other military personnel to make accurate and fact-based decisions after reviewing the information and knowledge that they have. Neither Americans nor the Congress have the full story about what is going on in Iraq – mainly because we are not there and are not living this experience with the troops everyday. Therefore, it makes good sense to me that since these individuals have chosen to devote their life to this profession – defense of the United States of America – they should be the individuals we trust to make foreign policy decisions. Another great thing about specialization in America is the ability of me as an American to know and understand that there are men and women with more facts, evidence, and intelligence on this subject than I have, and that they are properly equipped as individuals to handle the decisions that they face. This is one of the many benefactors of Capitalism.

CONCLUSIONS:

I spent quite a bit of time in the section on the Democratic Congress discussing their instrumental role in both wars the United States is involved in right now, and I do not believe that I have the knowledge or intelligence on this subject to fully describe to the American public how they should view these wars. This is not something you or I should feel we have the authority to decide. This is war. This is not pleasant and not a desirable outcome for anyone. But if it is necessary, then it is necessary, and as Americans, we will do what is necessary to preserve our way of life and show to foreign countries that if they step out of line with the United States of America they will be metaphorically smacked and literally bombed back into place. I believe that Americans should listen to their generals, commanders, and other military advisors that have dedicated their life to this profession and to seeing that we still have the most competent and effective military in the world. These men and women should be given this responsibility to decide what military progress means, how it is defined, and when it should be halted because they have gained that authority through their continued allegiance to this country. I am not suggesting that every single person be trusted, or that a single person cannot be corrupted while serving in the military, but this is not something that I worry about in my day-to-day life as an American. I respect these authority figures in the military that have dedicated their lives to seeing the continued national, domestic, and foreign security of the United States. But also, remember, that the generals and commanders do not want to send their brave men and women into harms way. They do not want to, but they must and are obligated to under the Constitution of the United States and the oaths that they have made to this country. They care for our troops and will see to their continued survival. I trust these men to take care of the United States Military, and they have shown that my trust can be placed in them because they are more than competent to perform the tasks they have been trained to complete.

I met a man, unfortunately I can't remember his name, but he worked on Air Force One and was a highly qualified officer in the United States Military – the Army – I know it's more predominant for those in the Air Force or Navy to be on Air Force One, but I distinctly remember him being in the Army. I really wish I could remember his name and rank, but I remember the man more than the rank. He was an older African-American man staying in a hotel I worked at as a desk clerk. He checked in for his vacation clad in military garb that obviously befit a distinguished officer. He was extremely pleasant and came back to chat a few times throughout his vacation. He told me about his voyage of sorts through the United States Military to become one of the very few men chosen for this specific profession. This was one of the most arduous of journeys I had ever heard. It was clear that only the best of the best in the United States Military made it to this man's level. His job was to transport and see to the security of the President of the United States at all times while traveling on Air Force One. He worked under Reagan, Clinton, and both Bush's. He called all the presidents that he had worked for politicians, but I could tell that when that man was on Air Force One his number one priority at any given time was the immediate security and protection of the President of the United States – no matter his personal opinion on the individual. I cannot explain to anyone how much this brief interaction with this man cemented my belief and trust in the United States Military, but it did. Men like these have dedicated their lives to this profession and have been shown by the military what true dedication, loyalty, and faithfulness to one's country means and can achieve.

The United States will continue to make foreign policy decisions that are unfavorable or disliked by others – especially America's enemy or those hell-bent on the destruction of this country. Americans need not be weary of the competency of individuals – especially American individuals -- to overcome any adversity or hatred that comes our direction. We will persevere against our struggles as we always have, and we have the intelligence in the American community to see that we never lose the freedom to be Americans.

Additionally, I would like to put another admonition in this book to Communists and anyone who believes they can eventually take this country over to Communism. The United States Military is not fighting overseas to free an oppressed country so that their own country can fall into the ruin of Communism while they are away. The United States Military fights for freedom, and anyone who threatens to take the freedom of Americans will be the immediate and ultimate enemy of the United States Military. Our troops and servicemen will come back from overseas if necessary to protect, preserve, and defend freedom in their own country. The Marxist movement strangleholding this country should not forget the lengths that American troops will go to preserve the very idea of freedom, especially for their own family, friends, and countrymen and women. You have underestimated the American public once again. We will not tolerate the direct oppression of our citizens by any enemy, foreign or domestic. The Navy has created planes that fly themselves (Call the United States Navy for more information), and the enemy does not and could not know about the technology and innovation contained within the United States Military simply because they are not supposed to. You do not know the weapons that Capitalism has given this country in our fight for freedom, but you should know that you will be shown if it is imminent that you desire to remove even our most basic and core freedoms — specifically, to free and fair elections, you will not take away the right of the people to vote for the person they believe will promote the well-being of this country.

Chapter Ten

Religion in America

I would like to start out this section on religion by stating that I believe in an unwavering separation of church and state. I do not believe the government should be involved in any American's choice of religion, nor should religious options be limited by the government. I also believe that the government should remain secular. However, that is not to say that the government should advocate the absence of religion, they should advocate the individual's right to choose which religion suits their lifestyle. The founding fathers desired so much for Americans to have the freedom of and from religion. So many pilgrims fled their country because of religious persecution. Religious persecution should not be condoned by the government. But I am speaking of religious PERSECUTION, this does not include voicing concerns about any specific religion. I will not allow the politically correct to manipulate my words so I will make myself as clear as crystal. Religion is personal. Faith is something that no Democrat, no Republican, no human period can take away from someone. A person's personal choice on faith is their choice. Some people choose to believe in Christianity, Islam, Judaism. Some people believe in reason, logic, and philosophical thought. Some people's faith rests in scientific progress. It is not our job as Americans to judge the faith that people have in whatever they choose to believe in because we cannot understand the factors that motivate people to believe the things they do. The only way we could understand this is to know all of the experiences, challenges, and situations that have molded one's life. That is why I say that faith and religion are personal and should not be a part of government at all.

Now, in a Presidential Race, all bets are off. These candidates will be scrutinized to their very last credential. Do not confuse this with discrimination or harsh criticism. If we did not look into the lives of those who feel they are qualified to be the voice and the decision-maker of this country, then, again, we would not be true Americans. A person's background will explain a lot about their upbringing and character. This is a reality that Americans must be able to understand. I, like many other Americans, would like to know the truth about these candidates' lives, no matter how much I may dislike the truth, I am better off knowing the truth than being fed a lie. And so are you. So here we will talk about the religious backgrounds of both candidates and try to decipher the truth through all of the media's misleading statements. We have been told a variety of things on these candidates' religious backgrounds.

John McCain was raised Episcopalian, but he now attends a Southern Baptist church (Pew Forum). John McCain has had a difficult time in his campaign converting the religious right to his cause. He believes in a separation between church and state and is private about his own religious views. He is outspokenly a Christian, but he does not espouse his beliefs as other presidential candidates have previously done. This has created somewhat of a divide between Evangelicals and John McCain. They have not voiced adamant support for his candidacy because they do not know if he mirrors the ideals that they deem to be important. However, I believe the religious right and the rest of the conservative base must look to the greater good in this election. We now have two options for the President of the United States, there will be no one else that can make the kind of progress these two candidates have made in becoming President. Now, it is time as Americans, for the religious right and extreme conservative movement to put aside their agenda for the time being. There will be another election that all of you will be able to voice your opinions on Roe v. Wade, the ten commandments, and prayer in schools. This is not the election for that.

We have entirely too much at stake in this election to let insignificant issues keep our conservative base from voting on November 4th. I'm not necessarily calling every Religious Right or ultra-conservative movement 'insignificant,' but I am saying that these concerns can be voiced through your congressmen, not your President. Conservatives MUST stand against Marxism. We must stand against Barack Obama's socialist intentions for this country because if conservatives do not vote en masse, then we have lost this election. The religious right must recognize that they will not further a single agenda they have unless they embrace a John McCain presidency. If Barack Obama is elected, the views and opinions of the religious right will be obsolete. This Marxist wants to 'unite all religions,' as if that is even possible. I sometimes find myself wondering if Barack Obama has even studied the history of religious wars and conflicts. How is the man arrogant enough to believe that all of these emotions and feelings that have been bred into people via their religion can be eliminated by Barack Obama's sheer presence? It simply will not happen, but I think the goal is more to unite people around Barack Obama, not unite religions. That's just an Obama Campaign talking point. Barack Obama is a puppet. The Ivy League education he touts so often has bred into him the ideals of Karl Marx and Friedrich Engel. He is an ideologue, in that he is a man with an idea and no real solution to follow afterward – except Communism or staunch socialism. The Communist Manifesto mentions the discovery of America multiple times and demeans the progress made by the United States as inconsistent with the ideals that they deem to be most important. Karl Marx and Fredrick Engel authored the Communist Manifesto. Just to clarify.

In the year 2001, 79.8% of respondents to the U.S. Census reported themselves as a Christian. 1.4% reported to be Jewish; 0.6% reported to be Muslim; 0.5% reported to be Buddhist; and 0.4% reported to be Hindu. Atheism/Agnostic/No Religion constitutes 15.0% of the vote, and the Unitarian Universalist constitutes 0.3%. These are the most recent figures I have been able to obtain to describe the religious affiliation of the United States of America. While I think this information is not necessarily relevant for government purposes, it is relevant to note that a significant portion of Christians view their ideals to be more aligned with Republicans. Specific religions may hold different allegiances to the conservative movement, but all of these Christian religions have a majority of individuals who generally subscribe to conservative policies and principles. While it seems logical that Christians flock to a more conservative ideology, those with agnostic or atheistic views seem to be more liberal. Those with an absence of faith in religion seem much more willing to put their faith in the government. But why should we trust an institution that on so many other occasions in history has been the downfall of individual humans? Individual humans that got in the way of government control have been persecuted for centuries. I am not judging any individual's personal choice on religion because I think it is the right of every American man or woman to decide what religion, theories, or belief systems will be most suitable for their lives, but I do think people should be weary of government. Do not let the government convince you that it always intends for the greater good. It may not. Americans must watch the government closely to ensure we never lose the authority to voice our opinion – especially an opposing opinion.

Barack Obama describes his religious affiliations throughout his life in the 'Call to Renewal' Keynote Address on Wednesday June 28, 2006. I will be taking direct quotations from this address because there has been so much speculation on Barack Obama's religious views and this seems to be the most accurate and comprehensive way to detail them – through the voice of the man himself:

"[Americans] want a sense of purpose, a narrative arc to their lives. They're looking to relieve a chronic loneliness, a feeling supported by a recent study that shows Americans have fewer close friends and confidants than ever before. And so they need an assurance that somebody out there cares about them, is listening to them - that they are not just destined to travel down that long highway towards nothingness. And I speak with some experience on this matter. I was not raised in a particularly religious household, as undoubtedly many in the audience were. My father, who returned to Kenya when I was just two, was born Muslim but as an adult became an atheist. My mother, whose parents were non-practicing Baptists and Methodists, was probably one of the most spiritual and kindest people I've ever known, but grew up with a healthy skepticism of organized religion herself. As a consequence, so did I. It wasn't until after college, when I went to Chicago to work as a community organizer for a group of Christian churches, that I confronted my own spiritual dilemma. I was working with churches, and the Christians who I worked with recognized themselves in me. They saw that I knew their Book and that I shared their values and sang their songs. But they sensed that a part of me that remained removed, detached, that I was an observer in their midst."And in time, I came to realize that something was missing as well -- that without a vessel for my beliefs, without a commitment to a particular community of faith, at some level I would always remain apart, and alone. And if it weren't for the particular attributes of the historically black church, I may have accepted this fate. But as the months passed in Chicago, I found myself drawn - not just to work with the church, but to be in the church. For one thing, I believed and still believe in the power of the African-American religious tradition to spur social change, a power made real by some of the leaders here today. Because of its past, the black church understands in an intimate way the Biblical call to feed the hungry and cloth the naked and challenge powers and principalities. And in its historical struggles for freedom and the rights of man, I was able to see faith as more than just a comfort to the weary or a hedge against death, but rather as an active, palpable agent in the world. As a source of hope."

In the first portion of this speech, Barack Obama notes his Senatorial race in 2004, where he ran against a man named Alan Keyes. He laments that Mr. Keyes told his constituency that "Jesus Christ would not vote for Barack Obama," and then later describes his reactions and anger to the accusation that he was not a real Christian. *"But Mr. Keyes's implicit accusation that I was not a true Christian nagged at me, and I was also aware that my answer did not adequately address the role my faith has in guiding my own values and my own beliefs. Now, my dilemma was by no means unique. In a way, it reflected the broader debate we've been having in this country for the last thirty years over the role of religion in politics. For some time now, there has been plenty of talk among pundits and pollsters that the political divide in this country has fallen sharply along religious lines. Indeed, the single biggest "gap" in party affiliation among white Americans today is not between men and women, or those who reside in so-called Red States and those who reside in Blue, but between those who attend church regularly and those who don't. Conservative leaders have been all too happy to exploit this gap, consistently reminding evangelical Christians that Democrats disrespect their values and dislike their Church, while suggesting to the rest of the country that religious Americans care only about issues like abortion and gay marriage; school prayer and intelligent design. Democrats, for the most part, have taken the bait. At best, we may try to avoid the conversation about religious values altogether, fearful of offending anyone and claiming that - regardless of our personal beliefs - constitutional principles tie our hands. At worst, there are some liberals who dismiss religion in the public square as inherently irrational or intolerant, insisting on a caricature of religious Americans that paints them as fanatical, or thinking that the very word "Christian" describes one's political opponents, not people of faith. Now, such strategies of avoidance may work for progressives when our opponent is Alan Keyes. But over the long haul, I think we make a mistake when we fail to acknowledge the power of faith in people's lives -- in the lives of the American people -- and I think it's time that we join a serious debate about how to reconcile faith with our modern, pluralistic democracy. And if we're going to do that then we first need to understand that Americans are a religious people. 90 percent of us believe in God, 70 percent affiliate themselves with an organized religion, 38 percent call themselves committed Christians, and substantially more people in America believe in angels than they do in evolution."*

So here I feel it is necessary to note that in the beginning of his speech on faith – Barack Obama first describes the voting trend in this country of Christians to be more idealistically aligned with the conservative movement. Why does he feel the need to discuss the demographic voting trends of Christians in the United States when he justifies his belief in his faith?

"While I've already laid out some of the work that progressive leaders need to do, I want to talk a little bit about what conservative leaders need to do -- some truths they need to acknowledge. For one, they need to understand the critical role that the separation of church and state has played in preserving not only our democracy, but the robustness of our religious practice. Folks tend to forget that during our founding, it wasn't the atheists or the civil libertarians who were the most effective champions of the First Amendment. It was the persecuted minorities, it was Baptists like John Leland who didn't want the established churches to impose their views on folks who were getting happy out in the fields and teaching the scripture to slaves."

I would first like to note how Barack Obama always prefaces a condescending remark meant to demean the people listening when he uses the word "Folks" in the sentence. He does it several times in this speech. "Folks haven't been reading their Bibles" is another example.

And I would like to define the political 'pluralism' that Obama refers to quite frequently because it may not be well known. Pluralism is 'a state of society in which members of diverse ethnic, racial, religious, or social groups maintain an autonomous participation in and the development of their traditional culture or special interest within the confines of a common civilization(Merriam-Webster).' Also, 'sectarianism' refers to the possibility of being 'limited in character or scope' or 'relating to or characteristic of a sect or sectarian.'

"It was the forbearers of the evangelicals who were the most adamant about not mingling government with religious, because they did not want state-sponsored religion hindering their ability to practice their faith as they understood it. Moreover, given the increasing diversity of America's population, the dangers of sectarianism have never been greater. Whatever we once were, we are no longer just a Christian nation; we are also a Jewish nation, a Muslim nation, a Buddhist nation, a Hindu nation, and a nation of nonbelievers.

And even if we did have only Christians in our midst, if we expelled every non-Christian from the United States of America, whose Christianity would we teach in the schools? Would we go with James Dobson's, or Al Sharpton's? Which passages of Scripture should guide our public policy? Should we go with Leviticus, which suggests slavery is ok and that eating shellfish is abomination? How about Deuteronomy, which suggests stoning your child if he strays from the faith? Or should we just stick to the Sermon on the Mount - a passage that is so radical that it's doubtful that our own Defense Department would survive its application?

So before we get carried away, let's read our bibles. Folks haven't been reading their bibles. This brings me to my second point. Democracy demands that the religiously motivated translate their concerns into universal, rather than religion-specific, values."

What in the blue blazes is this supposed to mean Barack Obama? I cannot believe that the next sentence after that is this: *"It requires that [the religiously motivated's] proposals be subject to argument, and amenable to reason."* Since when have Barack Obama's ideals and doctrines been subject to argument and amenable to reason? I'm serious. This is a man that refuses to have a true presidential political debate. He certainly has not had what could be considered an actual debate with John McCain up until this point – Obama, an actual debate entails you standing on a stage WITH your opponent and debating his solutions with your own. You have not done that so do not claim that you have had a debate unless you want everyone in this country to begin questioning your understanding of the term 'debate.' But the more pressing matter is that this man is dictating that Christians, excuse me 'religiously-motivated' individuals, need to always ensure that their proposals be subject to argument and amenable to reason? Barack Obama needs to learn to lead by example.

"I may be opposed to abortion for religious reasons, but if I seek to pass a law banning the practice, I cannot simply point to the teachings of my church or evoke God's will. I have to explain why abortion violates some principle that is accessible to people of all faiths, including those with no faith at all."

Huh? What is an example of 'some principle that is accessible to people of all faiths, including those with no faith at all?' Thou shalt not murder? I really don't know what he's referring to here – but I think it was meant to be intentionally vague. I also do not believe that Senator Obama is opposed to abortion on moral grounds. I will discuss an instance of a botched abortion and Senator Obama's involvement in that case at the end of this section.

"Now this is going to be difficult for some who believe in the inerrancy of the Bible, as many evangelicals do. But in a pluralistic democracy, we have no choice. Politics depends on our ability to persuade each other of common aims based on a common reality. It involves the compromise, the art of what's possible. At some fundamental level, religion does not allow for compromise. It's the art of the impossible. If God has spoken, then followers are expected to live up to God's edicts, regardless of the consequences. To base one's life on such uncompromising commitments may be sublime, but to base our policy making on such commitments would be a dangerous thing."

I agree with his point about separation of church and state, but I do think it is interesting that Barack Obama likens politics to the 'art of what's possible.' This is just another example of why he is an ideologue. It's not as much the art of what's possible as the implementation of what's possible.

"And if you doubt that, let me give you an example. We all know the story of Abraham and Isaac. Abraham is ordered by God to offer up his only son, and without argument, he takes Isaac to the mountaintop, binds him to an altar, and raises his knife, prepared to act as God has commanded. Of course, in the end God sends down an angel to intercede at the very last minute, and Abraham passes God's test of devotion. But it's fair to say that if any of us leaving this church saw Abraham on a roof of a building raising his knife, we would, at the very least, call the police and expect the Department of Children and Family Services to take Isaac away from Abraham. We would do so because we do not hear what Abraham hears, do not see what Abraham sees, true as those experiences may be. So the best we can do is act in accordance with those things that we all see, and that we all hear, be it common laws or basic reason."

I'm going to make an analogy now, and leftists, you're not going to like this, but you're going to have to get over it and grow a spine. Some things that you don't like to hear can still be fact-based and necessary for discussion. I think it is revealing that Barack Obama chose to cite the biblical story of Abraham and Isaac in this political speech. A father is willing to sacrifice his son for the will of God. Does that story sound familiar to you? I would like to compare Barack Obama to Abraham and the American people collectively to Isaac and then 'the Will of God' to 'the Greater Good – As believed by Barack Obama.' I have concluded that Barack Obama would sacrifice the American public if he believed he was doing it for the greater good of his cause.

"Finally, any reconciliation between faith and democratic pluralism requires some sense of proportion. This goes for both sides. Even those who claim the Bible's inerrancy make distinctions between Scriptural edicts, sensing that some passages - the Ten Commandments, say, or a belief in Christ's divinity - are central to Christian faith, while others are more culturally specific and may be modified to accommodate modern life. The American people intuitively understand this, which is why the majority of Catholics practice birth control and some of those opposed to gay marriage nevertheless are opposed to a Constitutional amendment to ban it. Religious leadership need not accept such wisdom in counseling their flocks, but they should recognize this wisdom in their politics."

It sounds as if Barack Obama is calling for people to put their religious values aside when it comes to supporting his policies. I would like to note how Barack Obama includes himself in pretty much any group of people that he addresses in this piece. He is a Christian, a Democrat, a progressive, open to any religion but freely addresses and criticizes specific preaching methods. He likens himself to the Democratic progressive movement in this piece when he discusses voting strategy. He said, *"Democrats, for the most part, have taken the bait. At best, we may try to avoid the conversation about religious values altogether, fearful of offending anyone and claiming that - regardless of our personal beliefs - constitutional principles tie our hands. At worst, there are some liberals who dismiss religion in the public square as inherently irrational or intolerant, insisting on a caricature of religious Americans that paints them as fanatical, or thinking that the very word "Christian" describes one's political opponents, not people of faith. Now, such strategies of avoidance may work for progressives when our opponent is Alan Keyes."*

I think the wording he uses in this paragraph is very revealing. He is speaking to Democrats in this paragraph, letting them know that he understands their plight when dealing with those of faith in this country. He describes that "we may try to avoid the conversation about religious values altogether," but why would he not be more than happy to debate his own religious values and explain why he would rather keep a firm separation between church and state? He then goes on to list a few direct quotations from Mr. Keyes that offended him and then laments on how he should respond to these allegations. *"And so what would my supporters have me say? How should I respond? Should I say that a literalist reading of the Bible was folly? Should I say that Mr. Keyes, who is a Roman Catholic, should ignore the teachings of the Pope? Unwilling to go there, I answered with what has come to be the typically liberal response in such debates – namely, I said that we live in a pluralistic society, that I can't impose my own religious views on another, that I was running to be the U.S. Senator of Illinois and not the Minister of Illinois."* My first point, Mr. Keyes was questioning Barack Obama's faith, not Barack Obama's supporters' faith. I do not understand why Barack Obama's response to allegations about his faith was to look to what his voting constituency would have him say. That just doesn't make much sense. Also, I'm Catholic, so I don't appreciate the Pope remark. But more than anything, I believe that Barack Obama on many occasions has shown that he is 'unwilling to go there' – and I think that is a poor example of leadership quality. He should have gone there. If he was so incensed about what Mr. Keyes had said about his faith, he should have said whatever he thought would make a good oppositional argument. I want a President that's willing to go there. I don't want someone who will stand idly by when someone insults them and then make remarks behind their back when they cannot argue their point or defend themselves. To be frank, I don't think Barack Obama has the backbone to be President of the United States – the most powerful and prosperous nation in the world. It's an arduous and pain-staking task. And not one meant for the weak of heart, spirit, and mind.

I also don't quite understand his position on the separation of church and state because at one point in the speech he addresses "the critical role that the separation of church and state has played in preserving not only our democracy, but the robustness of our religious practice. Folks tend to forget that during our founding, it wasn't the atheists or the civil libertarians who were the most effective champions of the First Amendment," but he talks at length during this speech about uniting religion and politics.

"And if we're going to do that then we first need to understand that Americans are a religious people. 90 percent of us believe in God, 70 percent affiliate themselves with an organized religion, 38 percent call themselves committed Christians, and substantially more people in America believe in angels than they do in evolution.

This religious tendency is not simply the result of successful marketing by skilled preachers or the draw of popular mega-churches. In fact, it speaks to a hunger that's deeper than that - a hunger that goes beyond any particular issue or cause."

So Americans are religious as 'the result of successful marketing by skilled preachers or the draw of popular mega-churches'? This was a clever attempt to disguise the sincerity and clarity of these words, but it wasn't quite enough to go unnoticed. Barack Obama seems to have a very 'secular' perspective on churches and religion. He relates everything about his religion back to politics somehow. But many Americans are not quite as flighty with their religion. Religion and faith are not contingent on public opinion to many Americans, and I'm positive that Barack Obama understands that the American public is a faithful nation. Faithful to one's religion, faithful to this country, and faithful to the ideals outlined in the Constitution. This speech just seems like an extremely superficial call to a crowd like that.

ABORTION

I was going to skip a discussion on abortion since I believe that it is a wedge issue because a Republican President for the last eight years has not made much headway in any real legislation regarding abortion – except to put forth legislation to ban partial birth abortion. However, I cannot ignore Barack Obama's stance on abortion or John McCain's attempt to grab at a pro-choice Vice Presidential nominee. Abortion should not be so far engrained into American culture that we cannot even look at the alternative of disassembling this form of murder. I once supported abortion up until the end of the first trimester, but I am mostly a pro-life advocate. The only arguments for abortion that have resonated with me over the years are that it is a crude but necessary form of population control and that banning abortion would have serious repercussions such as a massive increase in abandoned babies. However, the pro-life arguments resonate with me quite a bit more. This does not mean that I am not a libertarian because I am fighting for the liberty of the unborn child. I do not believe that the mother has the authority to terminate her pregnancy and her unborn child's life simply because she did not consider the consequences of her actions before she chose to engage in unprotected sex. Women, you do not indefinitely have the authority to kill your child just because you cannot or will not deal with the consequences. I'm sick of having this argument with people too. This is not a difference of opinion, this is a factual reality being ignored on the basis of political correctness. If the woman questioning having an abortion decided against it, a child would be born, would it not? Just because the child is developing and forming inside the uterus and is at its most weak and vulnerable stage of life, does not mean that it does not have rights to life as every human being in this country is entitled to. Here's a solution to your problem, women, if you want to continue to live like trash, then use protection. If you do not, then you will be responsible for the repercussions of your actions. No more hand-holding. No more coddling. I'm sick of hearing females whine and complain because they "had" to get an abortion. You did not "have" to do anything, you CHOSE to to get an abortion, for your own gain. Period. The American public can continue to sugar-coat the reality of these actions, and coddle these women until they feel vindicated in their selfish decision, but it makes absolutely no one better off to approach the subject of abortion that way. Abortion should be brought to an end because it is not American, and it is not humane. I have heard the oppositional arguments from women, and I assure you, I have very little respect for many of those arguments because they are centered around the idea of the mother's 'choice.' It's the woman's body and therefore it is believed that the mother should be able to terminate her pregnancy whenever she feels it is necessary. Absolutely not – unless it is a special circumstance involving the life of the mother. What do these women think gives them the authority to terminate this child's life without even giving them a chance to live? They don't have to live with YOU, if you would be an unfit parent; that's why we have adoption. Orphanages. These 'pro-choice' women talk in scientific terms they barely understand about cells and fetuses as if they are only that and are not forming something much greater than a cluster of cells. This is a child. Whether you would like to believe it or not, this is a child. I understand many women will disagree with me on this, and that is fine, but I am not compromising my beliefs in order to write a book. I disagree with abortion strongly and have strong moral and ethical obligations to disclose my accurate viewpoint on this topic. If you disagree, that is fine, I'm sure we agree on something else contained within this book. The real reason for this section of the book is to disclose some more information about the Presidential Candidates.

Partial birth abortion is heinous. I'm not sure if people that attended school in the north were properly informed of the practice because I do not see how any sane, moral individual could support this form of murder under any circumstance except the life of the mother. The Non-denominational Christian school I attended showed a video to the children in the 8th grade of this heinous act, and while I am forever scarred seeing the horrible image of a child being murdered by its mother and trained physicians at the time of its birth, I am glad that I was given the correct and undiluted information – even at a young age. Partial birth abortion involves the slaughter of a fully-formed fetus as it is exiting the uterus in preparation for birth. In other words, as the baby is being born, a pair of scissors are injected into the soft spot on the baby's skull, and the baby is killed. Apparently that is a somewhat outdated form of the procedure because I just read an updated form of the procedure, and it is painful even to read. They inject scissors into the base of the skull open the scissors and then suction the contents of the skull out of the baby's body as it is being born. If anyone would like to debate on the humane nature of this procedure, then you are not a human being with morals, ethics, or a conscience, and your opinion should not be valued because you clearly have no compassion even for developed babies exiting the birthing canal. Only a despicable human being would have this procedure done or perform such a procedure. People should be shunned from society for inhumanely and unceremoniously murdering an infant as it is being born. Why would anyone fight for this? We will see in a moment when I explain Barack Obama's stance on this particular issue. We must not let this practice continue in the United States of America. These democratic politicians will exonerate people who continue to engage in these acts any chance they get because they do not think people need to be responsible for the repercussions of their actions. Barack Obama has personally disgusted me in reference to his stance on partial birth abortion, and I will not let his despicable stance on this go unnoticed. It will be written into this book because it is important for people to understand the moral and ethical repercussions of submitting to this act and allowing it to continue indefinitely -- without regard to the life of the child whatsoever.

I will be referencing an article titled "Handle with Care: Obama's abortion problem" written by Paul Kengor & Jarrett Skorup. I will be quoting specific excerpts and then giving brief summaries and further commentary on the facts.

"In 2002, Congress passed the Born Alive Infant Protection Act (BAIPA). BAIPA is simple: It establishes that if an abortion is attempted on a fetus and the fetus survives — alas, magically morphing into a "baby" — everything medically possible must be done to save the child. Plainly, if a fetus takes a breath of air outside the womb, personhood has been established, and all persons in America must receive medical care from trained professionals on the scene. Americans are not to be denied emergency medical care.

Such legislation was necessary because of the countless number of times in which babies who survived abortions were not offered medical treatment after Roe v. Wade became the law of the land in 1973. Unknown numbers of these babies — unknown to the would-be mothers, to the medical community, to the general public — were left instead to die alone in a room, typically abandoned to a cold, hard, metal table, or in a trash can, behind closed doors, slowly gasping for air until they perished. Chalk it up as yet another glorious consequence of a woman's "right to choose." This China-like human-rights atrocity went on in America for three decades. Mercifully, at long last, Congress finally did something about it by introducing BAIPA in 2002. In the early stages, the bill was opposed by NARAL and extremist pro-choice groups, but objections ceased as a vote on the bill approached, most likely in anticipation of the public outcry. Yes, even the abortion industry can occasionally smell a bad p.r. move. The bill passed overwhelming in the House, by a margin of 380-15, and unanimously in the Senate, where even the most fanatical abortion-rights advocates — from Barbara Boxer to Hillary Clinton — were on board. The bill was signed into law by President Bush on August 5, 2002. In attendance was Gianna Jessen, who in 1977 had survived a saline abortion attempt."

Now why would someone oppose this legislation because opposition to this sort of standard entails STRICT moral and ethical repercussions? Only a person with seriously skewed moral values would support leaving an infant to die after it has been born simply because the mother and father do not have the courage to claim responsibility for their own child. I am disgusted that Barack Obama opposes this legislation. There is adoption. There are orphanages. There are many places in this country where good people will care for abandoned babies. Babies do not belong in garbage cans, dumpsters, storage closets; they do not deserve this treatment! These are babies! Sweet, innocent, newborn babies. Here are the facts of Obama's stance on this legislation put forth by President George W. Bush.

"At the time that BAIPA went through the U.S. Congress, Obama was a member of the Illinois Senate, meaning, of course, that he could not vote on the federal BAIPA bill. He could, however, vote on such legislation if it were introduced in Illinois, as was being done by state legislatures around the country. That opportunity came when legislation was introduced in the Illinois legislature.

Offering testimony on the Illinois version of BAIPA was an eyewitness to the horror of these "survivor" abortions: Jill Stanek, a nurse from a hospital in Oak Lawn, Illinois, who had witnessed several occasions of babies surviving attempted abortions and then being left to die. For Stanek, recalling these episodes is like revisiting a nightmare in painstaking, graphic detail. But Stanek saw her testimony as a necessary evil to what she figured would be a "no-brainer" for Illinois legislators. She would later admit that she had been "naïve." Her no-brainer met a major, unforeseen obstacle: a committee member named Barack Obama. From the moment of her testimony, Stanek sensed she was in trouble: She recalled an incident when she was asked to take an aborted Down's Syndrome baby to the hospital "Soiled Utility Room," where the "attempted-aborted" babies were sent to take their final breaths. The little boy's parents did not want to hold him, and none of the other nurses could find the time or bear the agony. Stanek remembers rocking the baby in her arms for the final 45 minutes that he suffered an excruciating life. "He was too weak to move very much," she remembered, "expending any energy he had trying to breathe. Toward the end, he was so quiet that I couldn't tell if he was still alive unless I held him up to the light to see if his heart was still beating through his chest wall."

This incident took place at Christ Hospital, which would fire Stanek for her testimony.Stanek was struck by Sen. Barack Obama's cold, non-response to her testimony: Interviewed for this article, she told us that he appeared "unmoved" by her testimony and "even argued against it." He told her, "What we are doing here is to create one more burden on a woman and I can't support that." Perhaps signaling his April 2008 remarks about his daughters, Obama could not imagine these un-desiring mothers being "punished with a baby."

Obama gazed right past Stanek's image of a gasping, dying, abandoned, newborn baby and instead saw an over-riding moral imperative: a woman's "health-care choice."

In Illinois, in order for a law to be sent to the full House and Senate, it must be approved within committee. The bill had been called up in the Senate Judiciary Committee — twice, in March 2001 and March 2002. Obama was a member of that committee. He first voted "present" on the bill and then later cast a "no" vote. It was there that he argued with Stanek's testimony.

But that was nothing compared to the more decisive obstruction Obama provided as chair of the Health and Human Services Committee in March 2003, once the Democrats took control of the Illinois Senate. From that perch, Obama prevented the bill from being called up for a vote. In fact, he even refused to allow Stanek to testify orally, though he could not refuse to accept her written testimony. No doubt, Obama must have considered Stanek too persuasive to be permitted to speak.Flying the flag for the "right to choose," Obama, as committee chair, ensured that babies who survived abortions in Illinois would not receive emergency medical care, and thus would die. As Obama obstructed, time ticked away, with abortion survivors getting no protection from the state of Illinois and those "medical" providers who swore a Hippocratic Oath. The gist of much of this has been reported, minus a few details. But what has been neglected is the crucial rest-of-the-story: As evidence of how Barack Obama did not simply oppose this legislation but was its primary if not sole hurdle, consider what happened to the Illinois legislation once Obama left the statehouse: It sailed right through.

In 2004, the people of Illinois elected Barack Obama to the U.S. Senate. This was wonderful news for abortion survivors in the state of Illinois — literally lifesaving. The act was reintroduced in 2005 and passed the Illinois House 116-0 and the Illinois Senate 52-0. Passage of the bill was more unanimous than even BAIPA in the U.S. Congress. Among the members of the Health and Human Services Committee that Obama had previously chaired, none voted against the bill in 2005.

Barack Obama had been totally alone in the Illinois legislature. His lone corner of support in the entire state was the small island of fanatics who make their living literally by killing unborn babies. It is no exaggeration to say that these people, and Barack Obama in solidarity with them, make supporters of partial-birth abortion look compassionate by comparison.It should be added that Obama had been commended for his obstruction by the president of the Illinois Planned Parenthood Council, Pam Sutherland, who averred, "The legislation was written to ban abortion, plain and simple. Senator Obama saw the legislation, when he was there, for what it was."

That, of course, is nonsense. This assertion was a classic red herring by the abortion industry. As obvious proof, abortion has not been banned anywhere in Illinois or nationwide with the passage of these laws protecting infants who survive abortions. Hillary Clinton understood that, as did Barbara Boxer, Ted Kennedy, and all of Obama's current pro-choice colleagues in the U.S. Senate. Why couldn't Barack Obama figure it out? Such poor decision-making, tragic misjudgment, or outright zealotry, is an important consideration for this frontrunner to become our next president — a man whose platform is about the future, change, and hope.

Democrats, who pride themselves on their alleged compassion, get angry and offended when their party is called the party of death. With Obama at the helm, they will do nothing to change the label. Quite the contrary, with Barack Obama as their voice, they are truly the party that has trashed the little guy.

Read through this document as it is a very concise summary of Barack Obama's instrumental role in thwarting this necessary piece of legislation, until he was elected to the United States Senate and subsequently left the committee. In Obama's absence, the legislation passed through the committee unanimously. UNANIMOUSLY, folks. As in, no one voted against it when Barack Obama did not chair the committee. I wonder why no one voted against it? Because it is a necessary, constructive piece of legislation aimed at saving live babies born to parents who will not take responsibility for their child's life or their own actions. Stop coddling these people, Barack Obama. The American public do not condone these kinds of unethical actions, and if you wish to represent the American public, then you WILL represent that view. Since you do not, you cannot be president. You do not have the morals or values to be President of this country. This situation also raises serious questions about his moral and ethical obligations to even the smallest and meekest of United States citizens. Barack Obama does not fight for the underdog as he has previously proclaimed. These babies are the underdogs of society -- not these uninformed, uneducated nitwits that oppose this kind of legislation for personal and selfish reasons. Who is Obama fighting for? These women? Why? Why would anyone want to fight for an individual so misguided that they would rather their newborn child be abandoned than properly cared for by medical personnel? Tears come to my eyes when I think of the mistreatment of these babies by untrained and unethical medical personnel and the parents. These babies need someone to stand up for their protection, and it will have to be those Americans that are not scared of looking politically incorrect in the eyes of ultra-feminists in order to do it. I am a woman, and I believe that women should have equal rights to men, but I do not believe that any man, woman, or transvestite has the right to revoke their own child's right to life. These egregious practices must be stopped, and a President like Barack

Obama will not put a stop to it, he will only further the socialist, ultra-feminist cause and blatantly disregard any obligation to the life of the child. Also, I think that more information can be found on this topic in Jerome Corsi's book "Obama Nation."

McCain briefly considered a Vice Presidential Nominee – either a questionable leader and conservative, Tom Ridge, who is also pro-choice; or a former democrat, Joe Lieberman. It seems that the conservative movement made a valiant attempt in dissuading him from choosing either of these men. He will do much better in this election with a more conservative running mate – my vote is for Fred Thompson, but I haven't heard his name brought up very frequently. We will be finding out John McCain's Vice Presidential Nominee on his 72nd birthday, August 29, 2008. I would also love to see him take Rudy Giuliani as his Vice President. I know that Rudy is pro-choice, but he is a good conservative and I would support a McCain/Guiliani ticket definitely.

CONCLUSIONS:

Faith, as I have said previously, is an extremely personal and genuinely internal characteristic of a person. I do not propose to know either of these candidates' personal religious views. However, I have proposed facts, specific excerpts of a speech, and my opinions of those facts. As an American, it is time for you to draw your own conclusions about these candidates. I do not mean from a religious perspective because I think relying too much on the religious affiliation of an individual can cloud one's judgment of their actual character. But on the character of the individual to be consistent and faithful to whatever it is they deem to be important. To clearly and concisely be able to lay out their beliefs and take credit for those beliefs. It shows the character of an individual when their views endure criticism, but the individual chooses to shrug off the negativity and make a more productive assertion towards himself or herself and those he or she intends to help.

Chapter Eleven

The Economy

This section on the economy was concocted before the revelation of the failing mortgage and financial firms: Fannie Mae, Freddie Mac, AIG, and various other banking companies. The economy faces a very serious recession and most likely a depression due to the actions of the federal government in purchasing these companies in order to 'bail out' bad mortgages and various other poor investments. It is important to read this chapter for context, do not focus on the fact that I agreed with the John McCain Camp when he said we were in a mental recession. We WERE in a mental recession; now we are staring into the future: not only do we see a recession looming, but perhaps even a depression. Take the economy very seriously right now because the government is attempting to seize control of major companies and financial industries, and they are not offering compensation to tax payers. The tax payers will by and large be funding this mass government failure. The socialist legislation the democrats have proposed is literally a direct insult to the American public's intelligence. We understand that the government does not have the Constitutional authority to buy out failing companies – hindering the market process and further denigrating the efficiency of the industry. AND, we know what happens to money when the government gets a hold of it: they fund mass government programs, they fund themselves (other bureaucrats and politicians), and the rest of America suffers financially at the hands of our government.

I will open this chapter by giving a brief overview of America's economic condition from the era of 2000-2006. And then I will list current figures from the Bureau of Labor to detail our current economic situation. The first section of this chapter will contain statistical data and numerical values representative of the economic climate. I will also compare statistics from the American Economy to the Chinese, Japanese, and British economies. I found a comprehensive article written by the U.S. Department of State's Bureau of International Information Programs. This article outlines specific economic figures and analyzes them into the larger picture of our economic climate. A very informative and well-organized compilation to describe the U.S. Economy from the years 2000-2006 – the article is titled "U.S. Economy in Brief."

"Services produced by private industry accounted for 67.8 percent of U.S. gross domestic product in 2006, with real estate and financial services such as banking, insurance, and investment on top. Some other categories of services and wholesale and retail sales; transportation; health care legal, scientific, and management services; education; arts; entertainment; recreation; hotels and other accommodation; restaurants, bars, and other food and beverage services." Further, *"Production of goods accounted for 19.8 percent of GDP: manufacturing—such as computers, autos, aircraft, machinery – 12.1 percent; construction, 4.9 percent; oil and gas drilling and other mining, 1.9 percent; agriculture, less than 1 percent. Federal, state, and local governments accounted for the rest – 12.4 percent of GDP. The most rapidly expanding sectors are financial services; professional, scientific, and technical services; durable goods manufacturing, especially computers and electronic products; real estate; and health care. Decreasing their share of GDP growth are agriculture and mining and some other kinds of manufacturing, such as textiles."* "Low-value, commodity-based manufacturing is disappearing from the United States, moving to developing nations where routine manufacturing can be performed at low cost," the Council on Competitiveness says (U.S. Department of States's Bureau of International Information Programs).

From the same article: *"The United States also maintains a trade surplus in services, $79.7 billion in 2006. The biggest U.S. services* *export category was travel by foreigners to the United States, $85.8 billion that year. In contrast, the United States runs a large and growing deficit in merchandise goods trade. While the United States exported more than $1 trillion in goods in 2006, it imported more than $1.8 trillion worth. By far the top imports that year were autos and auto parts, $211.9 billion, and crude oil $225.2 billion. The top sources of U.S. imports were Canada, China, Mexico, Japan, and Germany. Among the top U.S. exports in 2006 were autos and auto parts, semiconductors, and civilian aircraft. The top U.S. export destinations were Canada, Mexico, Japan, China, and the United Kingdom. In 2000-2006, even though U.S. goods exports increased 33 percent, U.S. goods imports went up even faster, 52 percent; the goods deficit nearly doubled over those years. The $758.5 billion trade deficit amounted to 5.7 percent of 2006 GDP, a level viewed as unsustainable by many economists because it relies on continuing inflows of foreign investment to pay for it."*

"In a free market, decisions about what to produce and what prices to charge for products are made through the give and take of independent buyers and sellers – sometimes a few, sometimes millions – not by government or powerful private interests. Prices set this way best reflect the value of goods and services and best guide production of what is most needed.

Americans also view free markets as a way of promoting individual freedom and political pluralism and opposing concentrations of power. *The U.S. federal government renewed its commitment to market forces from the 1970s on by dismantling regulations that had sheltered some industries – such as trucking, airlines, and telecommunications – from market competition for decades.*

Vigorous competition and a regulatory system that embraces technological change have made the U.S. economy productive and provided American households with relatively high incomes. U.S. productivity went up briskly in the 1990s, with a peak of 4.1 percent gain in 2002. This widened a lead over the European Union and Japan, mostly by more effective application of information technology. Since then, productivity gains have fallen off, only 1.6 percent in 2006.

A dynamic economy implies the freedom to fail. In the United States, business failure does not carry the social stigma it does in some countries. Failure, in fact, is often viewed as a valuable learning experience for the entrepreneur, who may succeed the next time.

In 2005 the U.S. government recorded the creation of about 671,800 businesses and the demise of about 544,800 others. Many small, little-known businesses start up each year; some succeed, some fail.

Tens of thousands of businesses enter bankruptcy each year, and some of them shut down permanently. In 2005 more than 39,000 businesses filed for bankruptcy.

Another measure of the U.S. economy's dynamism: Of the 12 companies that Dow Jones listed in 1896 when it created its famous stock index to represent the industrial sector, only one, General Electric, remains on the index now. Others disappeared from the index as they were acquired by other companies, split into smaller companies, became relatively smaller players in the economy, or simply dissolved. Some of the companies that replaced them started out as small businesses."

The U.S. Department of State's Bureau of International Information's program has produced a document with a lot of wisdom and knowledge of the ideals surrounding Capitalism, and specific analyses of the direct impact that this form of government has on the American mindset for success.

Capitalism is at stake in this general election. In the words of Mark Levin, economic freedom is at stake in this election. We are being bombarded with governmentally funded programs meant to stabilize but with this supposed stabilization will come government control. The American public is being fed propaganda and falsities by the mainstream media and members of the current Democratic congress. The policies Barack Obama holds so much faith in are, in essence, Marxism -- which has never yielded the kind of productivity that our Capitalist economy has been single-handedly responsible for over the last 232 years. The United States has the largest economy the world has ever seen. This is also in light of the fact that we have a smaller population than other countries subscribing to Marxist, socialist, or Communist regimes. Democrats would like us to believe our economy is floundering. That is not the case. The McCain Camp is right: we are in a mental recession, not an economic recession – Economists have not even labeled this a technical recession yet. But one thing many Americans may not understand is that the economy is cyclical by nature. There will be periods of growth and periods of recession. If these periods of recession are handled according to Capitalistic principles and ideals, then the economy will naturally begin to cycle towards economic growth and prosperity. People have forgotten Adam Smith's idea of the "invisible hand" guiding our Capitalistic economy to success. Many people may not have forgotten about it because they never knew about it in the first place. So I will explain the economic idea of the "invisible hand," better yet I will let Adam Smith himself explain it as he did in his book entitled "<u>An Inquiry into the Nature and Causes of the Wealth of Nations</u>:

"Every individual necessarily labours to render the annual revenue of the society as great as he can. He generally neither intends to promote the public interest, nor knows how much he is promoting it ... He intends only his own gain, and he is in this, as in many other cases, led by an invisible hand to promote an end which was no part of his intention. Nor is it always the worse for society that it was no part of his intention. By pursuing his own interest he frequently promotes that of the society more effectually than when he really intends to promote it. I have never known much good done by those who affected to trade for the public good."

Output per person in this country is much higher than in competing countries. This is an economically stable nation as long as we retain the ideals and laws our forefathers outlined in the Constitution – clearly such a magnificent work that it has created the land of the free, our America. This document is what has set us apart from nations that have fallen into chaos and ruin because of the corruption of their government. The government can be trusted to an extent, but it is the individual person that Americans value more than the role of government. Bureaucracies are fraught with long lines, unmotivated workers, functional disorganization, so why would we want to create more federally funded programs? The federally funded programs we do have in place are begging for more funding, and yet the democratic solution to the economic crisis is to increase taxes and astronomically inflate prices while simultaneously diminishing the value of the dollar and installing federally-mandated programs such as healthcare, insurance, free college tuition, free job training (even for criminals), wage insurance, free childcare, universal pre-school, more subsidized income housing, etc (Levin). How can the democrats complain about the deficit when their only solution for fixing it is raising our everyday costs to near backbreaking levels? If Barack Obama is elected, it is my belief that we will have another Depression. A Marxist will have very little foresight to deal with an economic crisis in a Capitalist economy. Marxists/socialists believe in a world in which the government controls the decisions you make. The government ideally should control the way you purchase your healthcare, regardless of the fact that the cost of a healthcare initiative in this country will outweigh the benefit substantially. The cost of a healthcare initiative in the United States is not just monetary; this initiative will also substantially deteriorate the medical industry as a whole.

The question Americans must ask themselves before they cast their vote on November 4, 2008 is should capitalism still be trusted to aid our economy in a time of recession or should we rely on socialist policies to fix our economic crisis? John McCain is a Capitalist. Barack Obama is a Marxist. He believes that substantially increasing all government programs will alleviate our economic concerns. It will not. It will create substantially more economic concerns for us. The government should be limited to just those programs that it has been intended to fund in our Constitution. Americans should not be scared of 'change' per se, but we should be concerned with undefined change that will create more federally funded programs for Americans. With these programs comes the Democrats perpetual inflation of prices and rising of taxes. This will not solve the economic crisis. It is so glaringly obvious that this will only create much larger economic concerns for the middle and lower class in this country. Americans also need to understand one important thing about Barack Obama and the United States Economy, he does not understand the Middle Class in America. He specifically will never be able to understand life in the South. He has never spent a significant period of his life in the South and he has made it clear throughout this election that he does not care to understand the concerns of Southern people – from gas prices, to religion, to gun ownership, to a general respect for our neighbors. These are aspects of the South that Barack Obama not only does not understand but would like to suppress because it will give him more control over our government.

Barack Obama touts that his policies will make the United States more effective and more competitive. However there is no firm basis for these beliefs since the funding he will require for his socialist policies will only increase the deficit – that is until he increases our taxes and our prices. Inflation is real. If you want prices to go down, then you will not vote for Barack Obama. Lower prices will be a thing of the past, a relic of a Republican administration, but further than that, we will not know what lower prices are with a Barack Obama administration. In Mark Levin's terminology, 'Obama wants to soak the rich.' Obama has claimed to be a centrist on the campaign trail, but he is actually far more left-leaning. He is the most extreme liberal in the Senate. Check his voting record – which has already been noted in this book – if you are unsure. Barack Obama recently gave a speech where he mentioned 6 times the idea of "economic justice." Do you know what economic justice refers to? SOCIALISM. Do not be fooled by different terminology. This is a Marxist at his core. He will hide these beliefs when it is relevant to his campaign, but after he is elected, it is an entirely different ballgame so to speak. Barack Obama referred to our current economy as a "winner-take-all market economy that Ronald Reagan created." But, wait, Barack Obama, are you sure that you understand and can properly reference American History? Ronald Reagan did not create our current economy, the founding fathers set that up when they drafted the Constitution. I understand what he is implying, but it is ridiculous to think that Ronald Reagan's conservatism was some sort of revolutionary attack on the economy. Don't get yourself all worked up, Barack. He also believes in "social justice and economic justice." What this means to you as an American is that Barack Obama believes in a mass redistribution of wealth. He will tax the rich relentlessly, he will target privately owned businesses, and he will inflate prices astronomically. This is NOT Capitalism or even a diluted form of Capitalism that would be mildly acceptable. This is socialism – Marxism specifically.

Barack Obama when running against Hillary Clinton made a very revealing statement about his perspective on our lifestyle. He was referencing Pennsylvania residents when he said, "Americans are clinging to guns and religion because they're bitter!" WRONG. Americans, specifically southerners, are clinging to the American ideals that have shaped our lives. Barack Obama does not believe in the 2nd Amendment right to gun ownership. Barack Obama does not believe that individual religion is important to one's lifestyle. He has proven that with his words, no matter the lengths he goes to after he speaks to cover up his true feelings. He has shown repeatedly that he does not have a grasp on the reality of the situation we are facing in the South and the suburban areas around the country.

This election has come down to a particular divide in beliefs. Small town vs. Urban area. Barack Obama is concerned with mass transportation, global warming, gun regulations, and many other programs that simply will not work for small towns and suburban areas. We do not want those programs installed in our towns. We want to drive our automobiles, purchase and own guns in accordance with our 2nd Amendment rights, the freedom to choose which church we attend, the freedom to voice our opinion even if it is unpopular and politically incorrect. There are so many ideals that Barack Obama cannot and will never understand about middle class Americans in this country.

The best solution to our economic crisis is to do the obvious things that will help our economy such as purchasing American-made products, limiting purchases to only immediate needs, being available for new job opportunities created by privately-owned businesses. Americans cannot continue to live extravagantly while simultaneously ignoring the situation we are in. AMERICANS can fix our economic crisis, but we must be committed to those solutions that have worked for this country so many times in the past. We must not cling to government-sponsored programs, socialist policies, and Marxist ideals, these will be the downfall of our country and will contribute to another Depression. These policies will not stabilize our economy, they will only exacerbate the situation at hand.

John McCain economically has voted in the Senate for the minimum wage law, for the extension of the Bush tax cuts, against a Children's Health Insurance Program funded by the federal government and a .61 cent increase in cigarette tax, and he also voted for a bill 'to cut nearly $40 billion dollars from the federal budget by 'imposing substantial changes on welfare, child support and student lending programs.' John McCain has been criticized as having a lack of economic knowledge. While this may be true to an extent, no presidential candidate has enough economic knowledge to aid the economy when the Democratic Congress is consistently and thoroughly thwarting it at the moment. John McCain as a candidate will support economic action by the government that will stimulate the economy and not inhibit it. Not all of his policies may reflect direct and immediate concern to Americans at the time, but if he continues to promote Capitalism, then his policies will help Americans in the long run. I do not necessarily agree that the federal government should cut child support and student lending programs; however, I do understand the economic idea that cutting some of these funding programs will help the economy because it will be less tax money that individual Americans must dole out to the federal government. And Americans also need to understand that federally funded child support programs and student lending programs are also not usually as effective as private programs aimed to support these areas (Washington Post Archives).

CONCLUSIONS

The best solution to fixing the American economy is for every individual to realize the critical part they play in the continued stability and productivity of our economy. If the economy is to flourish, then Americans must flourish. If the economy is to become more productive, then Americans must become more productive. If your industry is not doing well, then be the change that makes it do better. Even if you work a job that you don't necessarily care for right now, times are hard and everyone has to do that kind of stuff, but you can help the business itself succeed if you become more positive. Look for ways to improve your business because you are essentially giving this business the pleasure of your labor, so make sure they enjoy it. You never know, you might get promoted. The idea Americans should be clinging to in a time of recession is innovation. We must innovate in order to become more successful. We must reformulate interests and businesses to meet public demand. We must drill for oil. We MUST cut back on government spending. This is not only a time of recession, it is a time of war. Americans must unite and show that we are still strong and can rebound from any adversity thrown our direction. We will succeed because we know that America has given us the resources and opportunities to do so. Use your talents, put those talents into the American economy, and then value the product of your labor.

Conclusions and Endorsement

This is a political argumentative book about the November 4, 2008 Presidential Election. I have presented evidence, opinions, and facts to show my support for a particular Presidential candidate. I did not initially intend to endorse Senator John Sidney McCain III when I began writing this book, but I can think of no alternative after all of the research that I have done. The arguments in this book always seem to support John McCain as the 43rd President of the United States because I believe that he is a capable, competent individual, and even though I may disagree with a few of his policy decisions, I agree with his ideological platform and the intentions he has for the United States of America. I believe that he is a dedicated man and has devoted most of his life and career to seeing the continued security, protection, and prosperity of this country. He will make a valiant president, and as long as his Vice Presidential nominee is not someone outlandish, then I will be supporting his candidacy from here until Election Day. Since I wrote this endorsement for John McCain, he has chosen Sarah Palin as his Vice Presidential candidate. He has made some extremely controversial comments towards the conservative movement, but with this woman on the ticket, I will still vote for him. However, he should remember that the American public is extremely disenchanted with the monopoly of corruption in Congress – so pandering to those individuals will get him absolutely nowhere with his base.

I hope that this book has at least presented you with some facts that you did not know before. I realize that some people will not agree with the logic of my arguments, but you cannot deny that the logic exists. Please disagree, voice your opposition in a productive way that presents facts and evidence to support your claims, because if you do not, then you cannot truly convince people to believe in your standpoint. Find out what it is that you believe in and adhere to those core principles regardless of how any other individual may feel about it. We are all just individuals -- no one individual is better than another, but we are better off when we can recognize the differences between each other and celebrate those rather than attempting to stifle the individual to create a large, undefined 'whole.' We are better off when we, as humans, learn from each other – be it mistakes, achievements, or pain. So please, do your own research, be the knowledge and insight that your peers hope to see when they discuss politics with one another. Please do not allow yourselves, Americans, to become uninformed and tied to a specific political mantra or slogan – those slogan's come and go, but if you can find and retain core principles and values that you believe to be of specific relevance or importance to your individual life, then you can potentially persuade others to know and understand your viewpoint.

My Appreciation and Thanks

I would first like to dedicate this book to a person that has been my inspiration throughout the entire writing process. When other people discouraged me from writing this book because of bias towards the candidates, this man convinced me that there were people that would be interested in this information and that I shouldn't give up on a pursuit that I found to be very important. He has also given me countless ideas and insight into the topics in this book. He is my collaborator of sorts.

So I dedicate this book to Mr. Wilkison. Thank you so much for your encouragement and your attitude. You are my companion and my love, and I could never have finished this book without you.

I would also like to thank my parents. I would like to thank my mother for her continued and vigilant support of conservative ideals and her encouragement and praise of my writing. I would like to thank my hero, mio padre, my father, for being the kind of Capitalist that I aspire to be. Always weary of either political party, he is a moderate and values specific solutions more than party affiliations. "If everyone in this country was a moderate, and there were no extremists, then we would have real bi-partisan legislation." Thank you for always supporting me throughout my life, dad, and thank you for encouraging me to complete this book. It means a lot to me.

Thank you to the rest of my family too. I love you all, even the Democrats.

Thank you to my college roommate and long lost best friend, Miss Lewis, for debating with me in our 'box.' Without your insight and knowledge about these issues, I could never have fully formulated my own opinions on these things. I will always value and cherish the memories of us screaming political obscenities at each other across the 4 feet of room we had in our tiny dorm room. Without people like Jackie, who actually have the knowledge and intelligence to debate on these issues without falling apart at the seams, conservatives/libertarians could never fully understand and appreciate the mindset that forms these ideas. I commend those liberals that actually understand their ideologies and beliefs well enough to discuss and debate them.

Now, I would like to thank one of my professors at Wake Forest University for his outstanding teaching methods and the knowledge about the political writing process I gained from his class. Professor John J. Dinan, thank you for inspiring me to become a political writer through your continued support and extremely effective teaching methods. I had to write two 12-page papers in one of Professor Dinan's classes, but they were definitely time well spent because without those, I would never have had the ability to write and research these topics effectively. Another outstanding professor at Wake Forest University that I would like to give special commendations to is Mrs. Alyssa Kessel. While I know that Mrs. Kessel and I disagreed on some fundamental principles, she is an outstanding professor and I really enjoyed taking her classes.

Thank you to Mark Levin, Rush Limbaugh, Sean Hannity, Neal Boortz, and many other excellent conservative talk radio hosts for always reporting on issues relevant to Southern Americans and suburban Americans regardless of harsh criticism and the threat of closure by leftists attempting to stifle free speech. Your work does not go unnoticed in the political realm, and Americans really value your contribution. Oh and Mark, I am also an avid dog lover and will be purchasing your book "Rescuing Sprite" as soon as I have time for leisure reading.

Lastly, much appreciation to the United States of America for allowing me the freedom to become educated and informed about these issues that are directly relevant to my life. Without America's liberty, I could never have aspired to be a person that writes a book. But this is the good ole' USA, so I could and did.

Works Cited

The 9/11 Commission Report: Final Report of the National Commission on Terrorist Attacks Upon the United States. Authorized Edition. New York, NY. W.W. Norton & Company, Inc.

Ball, Terence, and Richard Dagger. Political Ideologies and the Democratic Ideal. Sixth Ed. Arizona State University. Pearson Education. 2006.

CBS/AP. "Bush Lifts Ban On Offshore Drilling: Congress Must Still Lift Legislative Ban Before Controversial Drilling Can Happen." CBS Interactive Inc. Accessed 20 August 2008. <http://www.cbsnews.com/stories/2008/07/14/national/main4257757.shtml>.

CDC. MMWR. Weekly Special Issue. "Deaths in World Trade Center Terrorist Attacks – New York City, 2001." 11 September 2002: 51(Special Issue);16-18. Accessed 20 August 2008. <http://www.cdc.gov/mmwr/preview/mmwrhtml/mm51SPa6.htm>.

Chapin, John C. USMCR (Ret). "Top of the Ladder: Marine Operations in the Northern Solomons." Marines in World War II Commemorative Series. Accessed on 12 August 2008. <http://www.nps.gov/archive/wapa/indepth/extContent/usmc/pcn-190-003141-00/sec5.htm>.

CNN Transcript. Anderson Cooper 360 Degrees. 11 October 2006. Accessed 20 August 2008. <http://transcripts.cnn.com/TRANSCRIPTS/0610/11/acd.02.html>.

"CNN debunks false report about Obama." 23 January 2007. Cable News Network. Accessed 11 August 2008. <http://www.cnn.com/2007/POLITICS/01/22/obama.madrassa/>.

CNN. "U.N. passes Iraq resolution on weapons inspections." Contributed by Jane Arraf. 8 November 2002. < archives.cnn.com/2002/US/11/08/iraq.resolution/ >

Crandall, John. "Henry Ford's Assembly Line." Suite101.com. February 6, 2007. Accessed 12 August 2008. <http://automotive-history.suite101.com/article.cfm/henry_fords_assembly_line>.

Fastest Cars in the World: Top 10 List 2007-2008. Accessed 12 August 2008. <http://www.thesupercars.org/fastest-cars/fastest-cars-in-the-world-top-10-list/>.

Friel, Brian, Cohen, Richard E. and Kirk Victor. National Journal's 2007 Vote Ratings. 31 January 2008. National Journal Group Inc. Accessed 11 August 2008. <http://nj.nationaljournal.com/voteratings/>.

Energy Information Administration. Official Energy Statistics from the U.S. Government. Crude Oil and Total Petroleum Imports Top 15 Countries. June 2008 Import Highlights: 13 August 2008. Accessed 20 August 2008. <http:www.eia.doe.gov/pub/oil_gas/petroleum/data_publications/company_level_imports/current/import.html>.

Engels, Fredrick. "Principles of Communism." Volume One. October-November 1847.

Eduard Bernstein in the German Social Democratic Party's Vorwarts. 1914. Accessed 12 August 2008. <http://www.marxists.org/archive/marx/works/1847/11/prin-com.htm>.

Erlanger, Steven. "Obama wows Europeans, but leaders remain wary." International
Herald Tribune. 25 July 2008. Accessed 20 August 2008. <http://www.iht.com/articles/2008/07/25/europe/obama>.

Haskell, Martin. "Second Trimester Abortion: From Every Angel." Fall Risk Management Seminar. Dallas, Texas. 13 September 1992.

IBD Editorials. "Barack Obama's Stealth Socialism." 28 July 2008. Investor's Business
Daily. Accessed 12 August 2008. <http://www.ibdeditorials.com/IBDArticles.aspx?id=302137342405551>.

IBD Editorials. "Young Obama's Red Mentor." 5 August 2008. Investor's Business Daily. Accessed 12 August 2008. <http://www. ibdeditorials.com/IBDArticles.aspx?id=302827467707515>.

Kengor, Paul, and Jarrett Skorup. "Handle with Care: Obama's Abortion Problem." National Review Online. 29 July 2008. Accessed 18 August 2008. <http://jarrettskorup.blogspot.com/2008/08/by-paul-kengor-jarrett-skorup-in-both.html>.

Krugman, Richard and Robin Wells. Economics. New York, NY. Worth Publishers. 2006.

Kulish, Nicholas. "Barack Obama's Popularity soars – in Germany." 6 January 2008. International Herald Tribune. 12 August 2008. <http://www.iht.com/articles/2008/01/06/europe/berlin.php>.

Lewis, Jone Johnson. About.com. Women's History. Edelman, Marian Wright. Accessed 12 August 2008. <http://womenshistory.about.com/od/marianwrightedelman/p/m_w_edelman.htm>.

Library of Congress Archive. "Advanced Bill Summary & Status Search for the 110th, 109th, 108th, 107th Congress. THOMAS. Accessed 12 August 2008. <http://Thomas.loc.gov/bss/d110query.html>.

Mghee, Morgan. "Exploring Realities of Offshore Drilling: NPR." 19 July 2008. Accessed 20 August 2008. <http://morganmghee.spaces.live.com/blog/cns!182233B6B71469E2!409.entry>.

Newser. "Nev. Union Bullied Voters, Clinton Claimed." 2008 Newser. Accessed 20 August 2008. <http://www.newser.com/story/16859/nev-union-bullied-voters-clinton-claims.html>.

Novak, Tim. "Obama and his Rezko ties." April 23, 2007. Chicago Sun-Times. Accessed 12 August 2008. <http://www.suntimes.com/news/metro/353829,CST-NWS-rez23.article>.

Obama, Barack. "'Call to Renewal' Keynote Address." 28 June 2006. Washington, DC. Accessed 12 August 2008. <http://obama.senate.gov/speech/060628-call_to_renewal/>.

"Obama stands by Iraq withdrawal pledge." 23 July 2008. Australian Broadcasting Company. Accessed 12 August 2008. <http://www.abc.net.aug/news/stories/2008/07/23/2311509.htm>.

Oinounou, Mosheh, and Bonney Kapp. "Michelle Obama Takes Heat for Saying She's 'Proud of my Country' for the First Time." 19 February 2008. FOX News. Accessed 12 August 2008. <http://elections.foxnews.com/2008/02/19/michelle-obama-takes-heat-for-shes-proud-of-my-country-for-the-first-time/comment-page-175/>.

Pew Forum on Religion and Public Life, The. John McCain. Accessed 20 August 2008. <http://www.pewforum.org/religion08/profile.php?CandidateID=3>.

Presser, Stephen B. "Reading the Constitution Right." City Journal. The Manhattan Institute. Spring 2007. Accessed 20 August 2008. <http://www.city-journal.org/html/17_2_clarence_thomas.html>.

Republican Study Committee. "GOP conservatives: Democrats' record is one of blocking U.S. energy supply." 20 May 2008. Special to World Tribune. Accessed 12 August 2008. <http://www.worldtribune.com/worldtribune/WTARC/2008/ss_oil0158_05_20.asp>.

Smith, Adam. An Inquiry into the Nature and Causes of the Wealth of Nations. F.R.S. of London and Edinburgh. Volume Three. Fifth Ed. United Nations. U.N. Sanctions Against Iraq and Human Rights. Economic and Social

Council. Commission on Human Rights. 5-30 August 1991. Palais des Nations, Geneva. Accessed 20 August 2008. <http://www.i-p-o.org/un-sanctions-iraq.htm>.

United States. Constitution. Cornell University Law School. Accessed 12 August 2008. <http://www.law.cornell.edu/constitution/constitution.overview.html>.

United States. Department of Energy. "President Bush Meets with Economic Team." Washington, D.C. 11 Jul 2008. Accessed 20 August 2008. <http://www.whitehouse.gov/news/releases/2008/07/20080711-4.html>.

United States. Institute of Peace. "Catholic Contributions to International Peace." 9 April 2001. Special Report No. 69. Accessed 12 August 2008. <http://www.usip.org/pubs/specialreports/sr69.html>.

United States. International Information Programs. U.S. Department of State. "USA

Economy in Brief." Accessed 12 August 2008. <http://usinfo.state.gov/products/pubs/economy-in-brief/page3.html>.

United States Presidential Address. Delivered by President George W. Bush. September 11, 2001. Accessed 12 August 2008. <http://www.whitehouse.gov/news/releases/2001/09/20010911-16.html>.

United States. Senate Select Committee on Intelligence. 110th Congress. United States Senate. 27 April 2007. Accessed 12 August 2008. <http://intelligence.senate.gov/activities.pdf>.

United States. Supreme Court Decision. "Second Amendment/ Gun Ownership." July 2008. Accessed 20 August 2008. <http://www. pccd.state.pa.us/pccd/lib/pccd/chairmanscorner/gunownershipfinal. pdf>.

United States. U.S. Census Bureau. Religion. Statistical Abstract of the United States. Accessed 12 August 2008. <http://www.census. gov/prod/www/religion.htm>.

Washington Post Archive. The U.S. Congress Votes Database. The Washington Post Company. Accessed 12 August 2008. <http:// projects.washingtonpost.com/congress/?nid=roll_housesenvote>.

Washington Post "The U.S. Congress Votes Database." The Washington Post Company. Accessed 11 August 2008. John McCain <http://projects.washingtonpost.com/congress/members/m000303/>.

Washington Post "The U.S. Congress Votes Database." The Washington Post Company. Accessed 11 August 2008. Barack Obama <http://projects.washingtonpost.com/congress/members/o000167/>.

Zeleny, Jeff. "Obama to Urge Elimination of Nuclear Weapons." The New York Times. 2 October 2007. Accessed 20 August 2008. <http://www.nytimes.com/2007/10/02/us/politics/02obama.html?_ r=1&oref=slogin>.